ESCAPING CULT ENTRAPMENT

Our Journey to Victory

GABRIELLA GALLO

WestBow
PRESS
A DIVISION OF THOMAS NELSON

WestBow Press books may be ordered through booksellers or by contacting:

WestBow Press
A Division of Thomas Nelson
1663 Liberty Drive
Bloomington, IN 47403
www.westbowpress.com
1-(866) 928-1240

Because of the dynamic nature of the Internet, any web addresses or links contained in this book may have changed since publication and may no longer be valid. The views expressed in this work are solely those of the author and do not necessarily reflect the views of the publisher, and the publisher hereby disclaims any responsibility for them.

Any people depicted in stock imagery provided by Thinkstock are models, and such images are being used for illustrative purposes only.

Certain stock imagery © Thinkstock.

ISBN: 978-1-4497-3839-6 (sc)
ISBN: 978-1-4497-3838-9 (hc)
ISBN: 978-1-4497-3840-2 (e)

Library of Congress Control Number: 2012901119

Printed in the United States of America

WestBow Press rev. date: 03/05/2012

PREFACE

This story of our family is one that has influenced and molded the characters of each and every one of us. Only until many years had passed without finding another story like it did I realize what I had to do.

Telling this true story means so much to me and my family, extreme as they are, I hope that you are able to connect with the events in some way and that you also see the positive side of the book. I am not a professional author by any means and my emotional ties to the events in the book made it difficult to continue and dragged the writing of it out over 10 years...but our story had to be told. Just before the final release of the book I became overwhelmed and changed the categorization of the book to fiction. Through the support and encouragement of my family, I released the book as non-fiction. Escaping Cult Entrapment is not only a story of a cult but a shocking and powerful biography told by me, the second of nine children about our inspiring fight through unparalleled adversity led by the fire and grit of our Mother and her two oldest daughters.

CONTENTS

ACKNOWLEDGMENTS

With love to mom, Elizabeth, who has always been there for me and provided encouragement. Thank you, Mom, for still having the energy to plan for and make special reunions and holiday get-togethers happen in the midst of your busy career. Thank you for being the single mom all those years, instinctively knowing how to nurture and bring out the best in myself and my siblings in spite of our hardships. I admire how you are still always helping others; you know firsthand how it feels to be without, and you "give back." Thank you for helping me with this project; I could not have done it without you. I love you Mom!

To my husband, Jeff, thank you for your love and understanding throughout the course of this project. I appreciate your advice and support with this exhilarating endeavor. Thank you for our wonderful children and my wonderful in-laws. It seems like I've spent my whole life working hard at planning and striving to reach my goals and achieve success. Ironically, with you there was no planning; it just happened, and I have countless blessings from our life together. I love you, honey!

To my loving sister and best friend, Lindsey Star, I've watched you grow up, and I cherish the times we shared together as little girls. I watched your marriage with my wonderful brother-in-law, John, grow and strengthen for over twenty years. I'm so thankful for getting to spend time with my darling nephews in the earlier years of your marriage. You are so talented! Thank you for the beautiful songs you write and sing. Thank you and John for all the family get-togethers you two often host at your home. Thank you, my wonderful sis, for always being there!

To Emily Knight, Andretti, Luigio, Sebastian Jr., Stefano, Madeline, and Annabelle, I can't say enough about how special you are to me. Each of you has a unique, wonderful personality and talent. Growing up with you brought such amazing dynamics and fun-loving family times to our lives! There is always something special going on with all of us, and Jeff and I look forward to our continued family reunions where we can share those stories and memories together (just like we did growing up).

Andretti and Sebastian Jr., I love hearing about how you surf and do all sorts of sports activities together, just like you did when growing up. Thank you, Andretti, for your special talent in the awesome music you produce. Sebastian Jr., you have always embraced life to the fullest, and it is so nice to hear stories from your daily life and, of course, we absolutely always look forward to hearing about your interesting experiences in your career. I love to hear about how you, Luigio, travel and meet interesting people all over the world. We value your creative art work and are amazed when you play us your classical guitar! I'm proud of you, Emily Knight and thank you for your encouragement during the challenging aspects of this project.

Stefano, your business success is something to be proud of and quite an inspiration to all of us. Thank you for always being there for our family, and for being a big part of my life.

Madeline and Annabelle, we always called you our baby sisters, but we are proud of the young, beautiful women you have become. You are great mommies and make good decisions in your lives. I can't wait to spend time with you and Emily over the summer!

With love to our cousin Lynn and her husband Joseph, our late wonderful Uncle Bob, and all our family members that have been a significant part of our life.

With gratitude and special thanks, to you, Randall. Being a writer yourself, you provided me with great inspiration. Thank you for mentoring me.

Many thanks to you, Shayna for your advice and support.

Thank you, Michael, Maria, Rick, Allison, and Stephen for your guidance and encouragement! Each of you provided a special support to me. They say things happen when the time is right; thanks for being there at the right time.

CHAPTER 1

Teenagers Meet and Start a Family

Elizabeth (Mom) was born and raised in the South. Sebastian Santino (Dad) was born and raised in Ohio in the 1950s. Mom was an army brat and always traveling. She had three older brothers and was not close to her mother growing up. She spent a lot of time with her grandmother and her Black nanny named Claire. They both loved Mom very much. Gram (my great-grandmother) was loving, independent and gave Mom the best care she could. Mom's dad fought in WWII and while her parents were still together, Claire took very good care of her. She loved to dress Mom up like a little doll in starched petticoats and hats and take her to Martin Luther King Jr.'s church on Sundays. Mom remembers very clearly that the preacher picked her up and brought her up to the pulpit and praised the Lord for blessing his church and sending a little white angel there. Mom learned a lot of old spiritual songs and used to sing them to us when we were little.

My grandmother, Fiona, was brought up as an only child at the time and actress throughout her childhood and teenage years. Her father, my great-grandfather, was an aeronautical engineer, and great-grandmother was a nurse during WWII. They lived a prosperous, comfortable life. Fiona was spoiled and lived her life being catered to by others. She was always concerned about how beautiful she was, and always wanted to be the center of attention. Her material possessions and her own personal appearance were very important to her. She ignored and neglected my mother, regardless of how hard she tried to get her mother's attention. No matter what, she was always met with rejection and criticism. Fiona divorced her husband when Mom was four years old (she has very few memories of him).

Mom remembers trying to spend some time with her mother while she was preoccupied with getting dressed up to go to a ball. As she watched her beautiful mother slip on her long silk gloves, and apply the last touch of bright red lipstick, my mother asked-

"Mommy, will I be as pretty as you are when I grow up?"

Fiona responded-

"That will never happen! Your ears are too big, and you have too many freckles. You should have been a boy!"

Fiona often made Mom wear boy clothes and never gave her little girl toys. She received balls, airplanes, cars, and trucks as gifts. Grandmother was more interested in herself and her three sons. Whenever she would visit friends and family, she often bragged about her sons without mentioning her little daughter. Elizabeth was often left alone and quiet.

> *"If you want your children to improve, let them overhear the nice things you say about them to others."—Haim Ginott*[1]

Fiona did not teach her sons to love, respect, and protect their little sister. One time, her three older brothers were being sweet to her, and prepared a "Princess Throne" and coaxed her to sit down on it. Although she felt like there was something wrong, she went ahead and trusted them and sat down on the "throne." She immediately felt a horrible, burning pain throughout her body. Her brothers started laughing hysterically as she screamed and ran away. They had prepared an electric chair for their sister. There was no

---

[1] Haim Ginott (1922-1973), a school teacher in Israel, a child psychologist and psychotherapist and parent educator.

one there to comfort her, the nanny had been fired, Gram was not around, so Mom's three older brothers were her babysitters and torturers.

Dad was the second oldest of seven kids, he grew up with three brothers and three sisters. His parents owned a family Italian restaurant and Dad worked there as a young boy. Dad's family was a traditional, old-fashioned Italian family. His grandparents moved to Ohio from Italy. Dad's home life was rough. When he was a young boy his mother was continuously drunk and he and his older sister were left with the primary responsibility of helping out with their five younger brothers and sisters. Needless to say, his parents expected a lot from him.

The Santinos (Dad's parents) opened their family restaurant when he was a toddler. They called it The Santino Family Restaurant and Pizzeria. Dad worked in the family restaurant ever since he could remember and his parents expected him to work long hours there. He would go there before school and work, then, he would go back home and help get the kids ready for school. His mother was sick or not around them so Dad would have to serve them breakfast, mostly either corn flakes with sour milk or cold pizza. And, he helped them get ready and off to school.

The Santinos wanted Dad to be a football player; they didn't want him to be a musician. They discouraged him from doing the things he liked involving music, like playing drums and pushed him to be a better football player. The Santinos had a tradition of having big family gatherings. Dad's family would gather around, prepare lavish dinners together, have parties, listen to music, and enjoy themselves. We have video of Dad when he was about 5 years old back in the day dancing in the kitchen with food everywhere and relatives all gathered around. Although his parents were somewhat dysfunctional, most of his family was close knit growing up and they stayed close throughout their adulthood.

Dad taught himself how to play the drums and became very good at it, he also taught himself how to play the guitar. His parents didn't accept the things that he loved. He loved music and after he met my Mom, he loved her.

1964-1967 Ohio

My parents were both raised in a bad family environment, full of neglect and lack of loving acceptance. My grandmother spent most of her time isolated from her children locked up in her bedroom while my Dad's mother spent most of her time either drinking wine or ill. Needless to say, when they met they both had a void of love and acceptance that needed to be filled.

One day, Mom was in her family's kitchen and she saw Sebastian (Dad) walk by with her brother. Dad asked Mark, "Who is that?" This was the first time they met. My Dad was in a band with my mom's brother; Dad was a drummer. They immediately connected and quickly developed strong feelings for each other. They were young teenagers when they met in 1964 and fell in love. Mom told us the story about our Dad's big Italian family who despised the fact that he had a girlfriend from the other side of town.

It was the first time Mom really felt loved; she and Dad had so much fun together. Dad's family owned a cottage by a river, where my parents often went swimming. They spent a lot of time there. *Batman* had just come out, and they watched it on Gram's black-and-white TV. They went sledding in the winter. This was a new experience for Mom: enjoying a friendship with someone who cared about her. She was fashion-conscious and loved to design clothes. She used to enjoy sewing and she made herself and Dad awesome, radical bell-bottom pants and outrageous shirts with exaggerated sleeves and cuffs and collars. She was a clothing designer in her own right, even way back then.

Mom also loved shoes and boots, and wherever she and Dad went, people thought they were in a popular band or something because they were always decked out. They were very popular and had a lot of friends. They would go to the downtown campus and skateboard at the lake. They went ice skating together, went to concerts, and won American Bandstand dance contests! They were inseparable.

When she became pregnant with her first baby, her mom forced her to quit school and moved her across town in a tiny apartment close to Dad's neighborhood. Mom was left there alone most of the time. Gram and Fiona visited her once a week to bring her groceries.

Dad's parents forbade him to visit Mom, but he did anyway. Fiona and Mrs. Santino (Dad's mother) took my parents to North Carolina where they could get married because they were too young to marry in Ohio. **Lindsey Star** was born. Gram bought her a nice rocking chair for their new baby. It had gold stencil on it and was well made, sturdy and comfortable to sit in. My parents were in love, but they weren't prepared to be out on their own.

Dad also dropped out of high school and began to work full time at his father's Italian restaurant during the day. He went to night school to become a hairdresser. Life became tedious and painful for them. The responsibility of being parents was difficult. They started to fight, and he started going out with other girls, which made Mom miserable. Next thing you know, she became pregnant again, with me, **Sophia.**

In 1967 Mom and Dad lived with baby Lindsey Star in an apartment in Ohio, and shortly after that I was born in 1968. Mom was completely in love with him and accepted him as he was; she didn't know what a father or husband was supposed to be like and didn't have any idea of how to handle the relationship or what to expect of him. They continued to have problems, and Dad quit his job at the family restaurant. He got his hairdresser license and started working as a hairdresser at a large department store.

Their relationship got worse and he moved out of the apartment and left Mom alone with the babies. Next, she had to move out of the apartment and in with Gram to help take care of us all. Not long after, Dad moved back in with us in Gram's house.

1969 Texas

Gram felt bad about Mom's problems and wanted to help as much as she could but she couldn't help to feel like they were off to a very rough start in their marriage. As always she was supportive and loving towards Mom but there was only so much she could do to help. Dad lost his job, and they decided to move to Texas where mom's older brother, sister-in-law, and other relatives lived. They needed a "new start." Mom had to leave her beautiful rocking chair at Gram's house.

He found a good job as a hairdresser and was considered the Italian stallion in the salon and became popular quickly. He was making money, taking care of his two babies, and had a loving wife. He bought a new car and moved us into a nice apartment in an affluent neighborhood, but he was still not happy. He had a void that still was not fulfilled. My parents had an active social life, they made new friends that would visit often, it would seem that this would be the happy ending to our story. Just then Dad started abusing drugs and alcohol and his life quickly spiraled out of control. They couldn't keep their new car which only made things worse. He became abusive to Mom and was getting high on drugs every day.

1970 Ohio

Mom packed up and took us back to Ohio and moved into an apartment with some friends. She got a job as a waitress. A few months later, she called dad to wish him Merry Christmas, and he didn't even know what day it was. He was in bad shape. She was so worried about him that she left us with a close friend and got on the first plane to Texas. When she got to the apartment, there was an eviction notice on the door, and she found him drugged up. She helped him get sober, packed up what they could, and moved out of that apartment and into an apartment in a rundown, low-income area. Mom decided we needed to give Dad another chance, and he needed us to be with him. She went back to Ohio, packed us up, and returned us to Texas again.

Soon, they lost that apartment and started staying with friends. During this time, Dad became very depressed. He said he had to leave, by himself, to find God. Our friends were kind and understanding, and realized they needed to help Mom. Dad left on his pursuit to find God. When he returned, the friends we were staying with felt sorry for us, but asked us to leave. Mom's brother helped us get an old station wagon and we then started living in it. Eventually, we bought a tent, and started living on the beach on Padre Island, then in parks. We would stay until we got kicked out. During this time, there were lots of groups of hippies that would hang out at local parks, and we started going to these parks because we didn't have anywhere else to go.

CHAPTER 2

Meeting the Children of God for the First Time

1971 Texas

Mom became pregnant with her third child, **Emily Knight**. Up until now we were together and survived the epic struggle of losing our home, Dad's multiple marital affairs and drug abuse. All of it just about tore our family apart. My parents were scared and didn't have direction, a simple product of family histories of bad parenting and difficult circumstances. They still loved each other and decided to stay together, but, they could have never imagined that the next single decision they would make would send them down a path sinking them deeper into turmoil and impact their lives forever!

Mom and Dad were 21 years old, soon to be parents of a new baby, and had two and three year old daughters. They were in search of peace, happiness and shelter. In early 1971, we found ourselves in a park in Texas with the **Children Of God Cult (COG)**. All the women seemed beautiful. They wore long hippie dresses and had long hair. They danced in huge, gypsy-like circles, while the men played their guitars, and the children laughed and played. It seemed like a happy, free-spirited, beautiful life! They approached us for the first time, and they talked with my parents and told them that God loved them, and that if they joined their organization we could benefit with God's blessings. They would have a place to live, plenty of food, and lots of fellowship with the other brothers and sisters who also lived there.

The COG were very convincing. We were desperate for all these things, so my parents liked the idea. They received an invitation, which had a map with directions to the commune, but they did not join.

The Children of God Cult was founded by David Berg (also known as "Moses David or Mo") in 1968. This was a hippie era when the idea of "love and peace" as a new way of life was everywhere. The organization was later known as "The Family of Love" or "The Family" and currently "The Family International". There is a great deal of information on the Internet regarding this Christian Cult.

For starters, "Berg called on his followers to devote their full time to spreading the message of Jesus' love and salvation as far and wide as possible, unfettered by convention or tradition, and to teach others to do the same. Berg also decried the de-Christianization and decay in moral values of Western society. He viewed the trend towards a New World Order as setting the stage for the rise of the Antichrist. Berg lived in seclusion, communicating with his followers and the public via nearly 3,000 "Mo Letters" ("Mo" being abbreviated from his pseudonym "Moses David") that he wrote or dictated on a wide variety of subjects. His writings were often extreme and uncompromising in their denunciation of evil, yet he always admonished the reader to "love the sinner but hate the sin". He espoused doctrines that some mainstream Christians denounce as heretical. However, his followers argue that his writings are permeated with a love of God. "Mo Letters" covered spiritual or practical subjects and were used as a way of disseminating and introducing policy and religious doctrine to his followers. He exercised tight control over his COG members through his Mo Letters and they were frequently distributed amongst the cult."[2]

A Mo letter Berg wrote in May 1971 called "Faith" shows how he communicated to the members and the writing style of his messages. Berg's writings were powerful and written specifically to persuade, manipulate and entice his members. They were unique as to how he wanted to make his audience feel and believe at the specific month and year they were

---

[2]   From Wikipedia, the free encyclopedia

crafted, he was truly a sick individual. These are some quotes during this particular time frame—

> "When you ask the Lord for an answer, expect an answer and take the first thing that comes. If you really believe and ask the Lord and want to hear or see, you won't be disappointed! And that thing you see or hear with the eyes or ears of your spirit, that's the Lord—and it will be such a comfort to you! Expect God to answer! Just open up your heart and let the Sunshine in!

> If you're really desperate and crying with your whole heart and are asking Him, He'll answer! A baby is such an illustration! When he's crying for his Mother, you wouldn't think of refusing him. Hearing from the Lord is our spiritual nourishment—and you've got to be able to hear from the Lord! That little baby has more faith than you do sometimes, 'cause when the baby cries, he expects someone to hear him. Because he knows—God put it in him to know—that if he calls, you'll answer. He expects the answer and he gets it! So you must expect that what you get is from the Lord.

> Shutting your eyes helps you to see in the spirit and to become unconscious of the things and people around you. Get your mind on the Lord and in a relaxed position where nothing distracts you, and expect then that whatever you hear or see is something from the Lord.

> When you cry, you must expect the Lord to answer. The longer you practice receiving nourishment from God, the more you know where to grab it and you just open your eyes and see it and reach for it. When you cry out to God for something, He pushes it in your mouth, but if you don't start sucking, you'll never get it. You have to have the faith to begin to pull. You absolutely have to draw God's nourishment. God can show it to you, stick it in your mouth even, but if you don't suck,

*you won't get anything. The sucking is the action of the faith!
You have to put your faith into action! Faith is a kind of
drawing power! It is you drawing power from God. It's kind
of like a bank account: The money is there and the Father
has put it there in your name—in the Bank of Heaven, but
you'll never get it—not one red cent-unless you're willing to
go to the Bank and sign the check by faith and draw on it!
But you see, the faith draws it! The Lord wants you to draw
on the Word—not only the recorded Word, but the living
Word. But it is you drawing and you must believe it and
start right from there.*

*It's so simple: you just have to have the faith of that little baby.
You just have to show him where it is and after you've shown
him, he knows where it is. And pretty soon you'll recognize it
when the Lord begins to speak. Some people get things from
the Lord and don't even know it is from the Lord. I did that
for years. I've been getting things like this all my life and for
a long time I thought it was just me—and all the time the
Lord was speaking to me. "I learned alone. I learned to love.
I listened to the still small voice of God." It just came like it
was natural—I didn't realize what a supernatural thing it
was—that a miracle. Just like the baby nursing—it seems
so natural. Yet it's such a miracle. Everything is a miracle!
Everything is supernatural because God made it all. If you've
got an open channel and tune in, the Lord will fill you—your
mind, your heart, your ears, your eyes! What the Lord is
trying to show you is that you can get it yourself! The answer's
always there if you're willing to receive it!"[3]*

Quotes from another Mo letter Berg wrote in April 1972 called "Be So
Happy";

---

[3]   Mo letter written by David Berg in May 1971 called Faith, from www.davidberg.com, The Family International

11

We all need a good sense of humor! "A merry heart doeth good like medicine!" God created us with a sense of humor and the ability to laugh at things that are funny. So I'm sure He Himself has a sense of humor, especially when I look at some of the things and people He has created and the funny situations He lets them get into. Someone has said that a sense of humor is the ability to see the funny side of a serious situation and to laugh at things when they're not the way they ought to be. God intended for us to enjoy living and He has given us the ability, the senses and the environment to enjoy it, including Himself, and our main purpose in life, as Martin Luther said, is "to love God and enjoy Him forever!

So God created you to enjoy the life He's given you and to love and enjoy Him forever and to try to help others to do the same! Even the martyrs didn't die sadly or sorrowfully, but singing and shouting and praising God! If there's anything in this World we're supposed to be, it's a happy people, because we've got more to be happy about than anybody else in the World! We have the happy love of Jesus Who takes all our burdens, carries all our cares, even lightens our sorrows; and even of our service for Him He says that His yoke is easy and His burden is light, and that it is the way of the transgressor that's hard! If you're finding His yoke too hard or the burden of His Service too heavy to bear, then maybe you're transgressing by not obeying Him, not casting all your cares upon Jesus, for He careth for you. "Cast thy burden on the Lord and He shall sustain thee."—Psa.55:22.

You're trying to carry too much and pull too hard! Let go and let God! Let Jesus do it! Don't work so hard! Just let the Lord do it through you. Maybe you're trying too hard instead of letting God do it by His power, His Love, His grace and His strength! We're not the Christian endeavor Union!—We're not "Christiantriers," but "Lord letters!" For without Him we are nothing and can of our own selves do nothing! So quit trying so hard! Let go and let God! Take it easy! Quit working so hard in your own strength! Quit taking yourself so seriously! Stop and praise the Lord and have a good laugh at your own weaknesses and ridiculous inabilities to do anything or accomplish anything for the Lord, knowing that if anything's going to get done, it's the Lord that's got to do it through you!"[4]

---

[4]   Mo letter written by David Berg in April 1972 called Be So Happy, from www. davidberg.com, The Family International

CHAPTER 3

Parents Join the Children of God Cult

In mid-1971, my family was at this infamous park again. When the COG approached us the second time, Lindsey had just turned four, and I was almost three. Mom was pregnant with Emily. The COG persuaded my parents to join them, enticing them with promises of food, clothing, and shelter. They seemed to be kind people, full of inspiration and encouragement for life. It was very refreshing for my parents and that short visit seem to sweep them off their feet. The COG prayed with my parents and they joined the cult. The prayer was a verse from the Bible which was commonly used when new members joined. The Bible verse reads "If any man believe Christ, he is a new creature, old things are passed away, behold, all things become new" (2 Corinthians 5:17). Immediately we were all asked to choose new, biblical names, which, the cult members explained, represented our born-again lives. Each of us chose a new name from the Bible. Dad's name was Solomon, Mom's was Esther, Lindsey's was Deborah, and mine was Abigail.

1971 Brenham, Texas

We were given a flyer with a map and directions to the commune in Brenham, Texas. This was the place where several hundred young people had found refuge. They said this was where hundreds of lost souls turned their lives around and decided to commit to serving Christ! They quoted the Bible verse "And all that believed were *together*, and had *all things common (Acts 2:44)*, they sold their possessions and goods and parted them to all men, *as every man had need*" (Acts 2:45). On our way to find the commune, it started to get dark. We were in our old station wagon, and Mom had made little curtains for it, and we had a foam rubber mattress in the back. My parents were driving around in circles and got lost. We ran completely out of gas.

Mom said—, "the car just rolled exactly far enough to reach the long gated driveway of the big white mansion on top of a hill!"

It was like a sign for us. This was where the COG lived, and this was the exact place my parents were trying to find. There were armed guards at the gate, which immediately alarmed Mom, but Dad thought it was cool. Dad rolled down his window and the guards told him, "If you follow us, you will be saved and if you give your lives to serving God, we can give you shelter and food, and you will become fishers of men." My parents were already familiar with what the COG offered, and we had many needs. We walked into this big, white mansion, and everyone welcomed us. They knew we were hungry—they already had food prepared and they served us. We didn't know what to say; we were so thankful for their hospitality. It was too good to be true!

All around us people were playing their guitars and there was laughter. We were welcomed with open arms and instantly we felt like we were with family. Mom always wanted her family to be happy and Dad was used to growing up with a house full of brothers and sisters and being around relative at gatherings. Lindsey and I loved to be around so many people that were happy and coming up asking us questions, it made us real excited to be there!

Lindsey and I were separated from our parents. That evening a leader named Ezekiel came to interview my parents. Ezekiel was a young man in his mid-twenties who had a vibrant smile with wavy long blond hair. He was fashionably dressed in hippie clothes and was quite handsome. In the interview Ezekiel was pumped up with encouraging information. He shared with my parents about the magnificent new life they had ahead of them and how their "new family" would take care of them and God would be watching over and providing for us.

Next they separated Mom and Dad, they said our family needed to spend time alone. The COG often preached that separation would rid us of our selfish, worldly ways. It started to feel uncomfortable and just not right to Mom, Lindsey and I. They quoted Bible verses to my parents which read, "Whosoever he be of you that forsakes not all that he hath, he cannot be my disciple" (LU 14:33), and "he that loves son or daughter more than me, is not worthy of me, he that loves mother or father more than me is not worthy of me, he that takes not up his cross daily and follows after me, is not worthy of me" (MT 10:36, 37, 38). The leaders then proceeded with their classic ritual and took our vehicle and all our belongings and distributed them among the COG members.

The COG practiced expert brainwashing techniques to obtain and sustain their objective. In 1971 there was an anti-cult group founded called "FREECOG" or "Free the Children of God" (originally named The Parents Committee to Free Our Children from the Children of God). This was the first organized anti-cult group that was formed in response to mind control techniques used by the Children of God. One of the founders was the pioneer of "deprogramming" (from Wikipedia, the free encyclopedia). "FREECOG accused the Children of God of brainwashing and used various methods including conservatorship and deprogramming to counter the group. By the mid 1970's, as the Children of God and other new religious movements grew and expanded around the world, a wider anti-cult movement developed in North America, Western Europe, and elsewhere. In the early 1980s many of the parent groups merged into what became known as the Cult Awareness Network (from Wikipedia, the free encyclopedia).

They must have singled out my Dad because almost immediately they had a plan for him. Dad was taken to the men's section in a private room and Mom was taken to a tent outside the house. They said they didn't have anywhere else for Mom inside the house. It was a small, canvas tent with a small, wooden fruit crate that was turned upside down to be used as a little table. There was a candle and matches, a small bed roll, and a Bible. Mom told me-

"I was scared. I saw lots of tarantulas crawling up the outside of the tent in the moonlight."

Our parents were told that they had to demonstrate their faith if they wanted to stay and become true disciples of Christ. Also, that they had to put their faith into action. A leader named Amminadab[5] quoted the Bible verse, "Trust in God with all your heart and lean not unto your own understanding" (Proverbs 3:5). Another leader named Jaazaniah[6] told my parents-

"The Devil will test you, and your true belief would be known to all."

But my parents still didn't really know what all this meant. The COG said if we didn't pass the tests, it would show we did not have faith, and they quoted the Bible verse, "According to their own faith, let it be done unto them" (MK 9:29 and MK 11:22).

That night, Mom heard Lindsey and me screaming and crying, and she couldn't stand it. She ran into the house and didn't know where we were. She followed our cries and it lead her into a huge room that had big double white doors. As the crying got louder, she knew she was on the right track. She was approached by two stern-faced women. One of the women named Tamar asked her-

"Where do you think you are going?"

Mom said, "I heard my daughters Lindsey and Sophia crying, and realized that they must need me"

---

[5] The Bible name Amminadab has two elements; one of them means make willing, incite, 'an uncompelled and free movement of the will unto divine service or sacrifice,' says HAW Theological Wordbook of the Old Testament, by ChristianEducation.com.

[6] The name Jaazaniah is mentioned several places in the Bible. Jaazaniah, son of the Maacathite, is among the leaders of the people who stayed in Judah after the bulk of the people were deported to Babylon (2 Kings 25:23, by ChristianEducation.com.

"Those two little girls are not your daughters, and their names are not Lindsey and Sophia. They are the Lord's children and have new names, new lives, and a new family! God will deal with them as he sees fit; do not interfere."

"I want my daughters *now*!"

She busted the doors open and saw us. Another woman was holding me as I was screaming. Mom yelled, "Give me my daughter," and the woman replied,

"This is not your child; she is the Lord's. The Lord giveth and the Lord taketh away; blessed be the name of the Lord."

The COG had strict rules that anyone who was disobedient should immediately be reported. The names of disobedient, rebellious people were passed down throughout the leadership so that they could keep an eye on them (they were considered to have a lack of faith). The leadership said, "To associate with these disobedient people as disciples, was being unequally yoked with sinners."

During this time, Dad was busy hanging out with the men and showing off his skilled guitar playing, which made him instantly popular. This was the first time that he really enjoyed playing his music in a crowd of people that all shared the same interest and passion for music. He was also learning the new COG songs, and they were teaching him about how to live his new life and rule his family.

They told him about witnessing. Witness or witnessing was when the members would talk to any worldly person they met about Christ. They would ask these people if they would like to say a prayer and ask Jesus to come into their hearts so that they could be saved right there on the spot.

In the early 1970s David Berg wrote a passage in one of his Mo letters about witnessing-

"Soul winning is not our major task! Witnessing his wonder working words to the world is our major task! Witnessing's more important than winning! We'll win very few compared to the millions to whom we'll witness. But we're more responsible to give them all God's message than we are to win them, for only His Spirit can win. We can only witness! What they do with our witness is up to them, as each must make his own decision. Even God can't win them all, but He wants to give them all a chance. We must give them that opportunity with our witness of His wonder working words to all the world!—And yet the world waits! We have still not given His wonder working words to a waiting world!"[7]

Later in early 1973 Berg introduced the term "litness" to his members. He informed the members that their job was to "litness". This term was similar to witness but had additional meaning which was *to* distribute his *literature* while witnessing. Most often they would stand at a street light corner with the tri-fold pamphlets (Mo letters), soliciting for donations. Berg's letter aggressively aimed at persuading his members to distribute his literature. The anti-cult organization called "XFamily" provides accurate information regarding the Children of God Cult. They provide information that quotes the original Mo letters.

More quotes (twisted insane messages) form the Mo letters;

"THE CHILDREN OF GOD WERE WORLD NEWS IN 1972! Their Jesus Revolution made the front pages and radio and TV around the world! Scores of books and magazines have been published about us, and some even against us. THE WORLD HAS HEARD ABOUT US— NOW THEY WANT TO HEAR FROM US! What made us world news? We've proven it can be done, and we have done it! We're proven it works, and we've worked it! What

---

[7] Passage from a Mo letter written by David Berg in the early 1970s, provided by XFamily.org

> *more proof can we have than that it works! Jesus works!*
> *His method works! His message works! His words work! We*
> *have a worldwide work to prove it! We have shown our*
> *faith by our works! His words did the work! NOW WE*
> *NEED TO GET THESE WORDS THAT WORK TO*
> *THE WHOLE WORLD! They've heard about us—they*
> *need to hear from us! Every word we tell the world will*
> *have weight, because they now know our works and words*
> *have worked! Our words have worked, God's words!"*[8]

The next day Mom found Dad, and she was desperate to tell him about what had happened to us, and that they needed to leave right away. But, to her dismay, he had already been *warned*. Dad was told our mother had no faith and was a sinner. He told Mom that because she was a sinner and had no faith, he could not be in "fellowship" with her, and quoted that "light hath no fellowship with darkness" (I John 1:6 and II COR 6:14), and she was in the darkness.

The COG had very strict rules. If you did not obey the rules, there were grave consequences. New members could not speak to each other, or anyone else for that matter. We were only to greet each other with holy words or phrases such as, praise the Lord, hallelujah, or God bless you. We were assigned to tribes. There were twelve tribes, and each consisted of twelve people. The tribes were named after the twelve tribes of Israel. We had to meet with our tribes each morning for prayer, devotions, and lessons about how to witness to "systemites."

"Systemite" is the word they used to refer to people not in the cult. It referred to people who had normal jobs, children who went to normal schools, and families who attended public churches. Systemites were also known as "worldly people". They were the people that lived in the system, as opposed to the cult.

---

[8] Another passage from a Mo letter written by David Berg in the early 1970s, provided by XFamily.org

Members were required to win new members and were given a list of rules to obey, along with our daily schedule and duties. We were assigned a daily buddy, one buddy to each member. The buddy system came from the verse in the Bible that says, "Jesus sent his disciples out two by two, so that if one should fall, he had his brother to lift him up" (MK 6:7-13). A buddy was a brother or sister who had proven to be loyal, faithful, and spiritually strong. The role of the buddy was to ensure that new members did not disobey, try to run away, murmur, complain, or cause any doubts in other new members.

The buddies were also instructed to encourage new members to write letters to their worldly families and ask them for money to support God's work. The letters were then put in envelopes, addressed, and handed over to the leaders to be proofread. Members had no postage stamps. The leaders would then mail the letters once they approved them. If members received mail, they had to open the mail in front of the leaders. The leaders read the letter before the member. If the letter contained money, it was automatically given to the leaders.

Members were bound to the colony and could not leave until they were deemed worthy enough to go witnessing. Even when they received donations, they were not allowed to spend a dime. The buddies would act like your friends—you thought you could trust them and tell them anything that was on your mind. Mom felt like she could trust her buddy, and told her she was unhappy and doubted that the COG were truly of God. She felt that she could speak her mind, so she did. Her buddy took this confidential information back to the leaders, and they sent for Mom. They rebuked her in front of everyone by quoting Bible verses at her.

They told her she could choose to leave, but that her husband wanted to stay, and she could not take the children. She was also told that she could not take any of her belongings, not even her car. They threatened her and told a story of another young mom who had been faithless and had chosen to leave. As soon as she walked out on the highway to hitchhike, she was hit by a semi truck and killed. And they quoted the Bible verse, "God's wrath shall abide upon her."

The men and women were always separated, but spouses were allowed to come together for dinner and participate together in the evening's spiritual events, such as "Inspiration." Inspiration was a time when all would gather together and pray, sing COG songs, and dance like gypsies. This was the only recreation the COG allowed, and it was something we all looked forward to. Those who were in trouble, so to speak, were forbidden to go to Inspiration. We would be at Inspiration and see our mom peeking around the corner from another room to look at us. Mom caught on real quick and became very obedient and earned her privileges back so that she could be a part of her family again.

We were told the Mo letters were words spoken from God directly to Berg (a.k.a. Moses David), "God's true end-time prophet." His words would then be transcribed by Maria, "God's anointed scribe," and were then copied and sent to every single COG colony or commune throughout the world to be read out loud to the disciples during Inspiration. We were told that we were God's end-time disciples, we were "The 144,000" described in the Book of Revelations.

There was an extremely strict chain of command within the COG. Becoming a leader was a goal that every member strived toward. Leaders had more privileges: better food, clothing, housing, etc. Every colony had a shepherd; two or more colonies had a district shepherd; two or more districts had a bishop. Two or more bishops formed a bishopric that was governed by an archbishop, and then the highest leader was the founder, David Berg (Moses David).

It was the responsibility of every shepherd to send reports through the mail. The reports included statistics of membership numbers, monetary contributions, and a summary of each person who lived in the colony and their progress. Anyone who was a problem, or sewed discord among the brethren, was also reported openly for all to see and the Bible verse commonly quoted was, "Those that sin, rebuke before all so that others also may fear" (I TIM 5:20). Mom developed a reputation within the Zion Colony, where we lived as someone to "watch out" for.

We gathered in large circles and had Bible studies for hours and hours and hours (oh, and did I mention more hours?) each day. Some of the parents and older kids learned how to play the guitar; Mom and Lindsey learned how to play, too. Lindsey picked it up right away and she had fun singing and playing the guitar with Mom and Dad. During Inspiration, we all sang and danced in circles together. Dad was a drummer and was really good at singing and playing musical instruments; he was very popular and they said he was becoming an inspirational leader.

During the work period, the women and older children got together in the kitchen and fixed large meals from the food that had been donated from stores and restaurants; there was so much food. Grocery stores and markets would donate truckloads of fruits and vegetables. We never really knew it at that time, but a lot of the food we received was food that restaurants had thrown away in dumpsters. One of the daily routines was to send men out to nearby towns to get food from grocery stores, Kentucky Fried Chicken restaurants and fast food dumpsters.

One evening, a young man was carrying a huge pot of stew that was really too large and heavy for him. As he approached the table to set it down, my sister bumped into him, spilling the hot stew on her head, and it spilled over her face and down her body. She screamed a bloodcurdling scream, and a large crowd gathered around her and laid hands on her in prayer. Mom rushed over to her and pulled her away from the crowd and put her under a shower of cold water. Lindsey stopped crying, and did not seem to be in pain as Mom dried her off. The members said-

"Praise God for the miraculous healing"

The leaders told Mom that her faith in God was growing.

We prayed together all the time about everything and became aware that God provided all of our needs, according to his riches and glory, in Christ

Jesus. We never took anything for granted. We were conservative in some ways, taught to use only two sheets of toilet paper, never any more. We were taught to take cold "army showers" and wipe the water off with our hands first, and then use only a tiny wash cloth to dry off. The women had to wear long dresses and were not allowed to wear makeup, perfume, jewelry, or underwear, and they grew their hair long. *The hypocrisy in all this was that the cult combined a focus on watching biblical movies and daily prayer with their own set of depraved rules.*

Before breakfast each morning, we stood in a huge circle around the table and all held hands. We asked Jesus to walk with us, guide us throughout the day, and provide for us. We prayed at lunch and asked Jesus to watch over the brethren and help them return safely with lots of blessings from witnessing. We prayed at night on our hands and knees. Everyone learned to pray, and we all took turns, so if there was someone that needed to practice, we could give them advice on how to pray better. The small children learned to be very quiet when someone was praying. We were happy that we lived there and loved the fellowship.

After a few months at the Zion Colony, our Dad told us that we had been proven worthy of moving to help pioneer a new colony in a different state. Our parents felt honored and they were thrilled. As we prepared spiritually, our mom felt as though she had really blossomed into a positive and helpful sister in Christ. The leaders started to see a big change in her and trusted her with this great responsibility. There would be other young mothers and small children at the new colony who would need her help, guidance, and direction.

The preparation for our journey did not take long. A big school bus had been donated, and we loaded it up with food, used clothing, blankets, and Bibles. Off we went, a bus load of ex-drug addicts, degenerates, society's rejects, young children, and pregnant women. Jacob was the leader and main driver, and Dad helped him. As we drove along in our old school bus without air conditioning or heat, we managed to be happy. We sang songs and honked the horn to the beat of the music. We sang "Honk honk, hallelujah, hallelujah, hallelujah, honk honk, hallelujah, hallelujah,

hallelujah, honk honk, honk honk, honk honk! It's a revolution, revolution for Jeeeeesus, revolution for Jesus, revolution for Jeeeeesus!"

People rolled down their windows as we drove along and asked how they could join us. We would pull over and tell them how they had to "forsake all:" quit their jobs, give up all their worldly goods, and follow Jesus. In the few days it took us to travel to Colorado Springs, we must have recruited at least thirty or forty new members, including some small, young families. Once we reached Colorado, the witness teams hit the streets and parks with huge displays of gypsy-like dancing, and singing. Hippies were joining us day and night, and our little group soon grew to hundreds! We were the 144,000 . . . . We sang the song with conviction and faith, "We're the 144,000, we're the 144,000 . . . Who else could be but us? Who else could be but us?"

1971 Children of God dancing gypsy style at the park

1971 Children of God multi-family arrival to Colorado

Santinos on the Children of God Bus on the way to Colorado

CHAPTER 4

Cult Discord and Final Abandonment

1971 Colorado

After we moved to Colorado Springs, we pioneered and established a commune in a large deer lease in Woodland Park, Colorado. When we got to the camp, there were other new families that had arrived at the same time. These families came from another Texas colony, and they were considered to be very important spiritual leaders. There were several hundred members at this Colorado colony: people were everywhere. It was wall-to-wall sleeping bags all over the place at night. As the Bible said, "people were added to the church daily." The leaders, as they had been taught, separated the husbands from the wives, and the children from their parents. Of course this was the way for them to reprogram the families and was how the leaders controlled and manipulated the members. Mom didn't agree with that strategy and rebelled against the leadership, which landed her in trouble with the new leadership. Once again, her position and privileges were taken away from her.

The children were placed in a house about a mile away from where the parents lived. Mom was really tired, desperate, and pregnant with Emily; she didn't know what to do. She was furious that they had separated us from her again. Mom told the leaders, "I want to go see my children," but they just ignored her and told her she was going against God's will. The male leaders who reported to the founder, Berg, made up all the rules.

They were hard, cruel, and they did not care that they were tearing families apart. Why didn't they listen when they heard mothers cry out for their children and wives beg their husbands not to leave?

Mom was wearing her only dress: it was a white-and-blue Indian print dress that gathered with elastic at the neckline and right above her waist. Mom called it an empire waist dress. One evening, shortly after we got settled into the new commune, she decided that she was going to stay with us no matter what, so she put on her hat, coat, and scarf. She snuck outside alone and started walking in the dark with a flashlight down a steep hillside, in the snow, toward the building where she thought Lindsey and I were being held. Mom later told us,

"It was freezing cold that night, and I was slipping and falling, scraping my legs on the way to the house. I could have miscarried or gone into premature labor."

When she reached the house, she entered the front door and we looked up and saw her right away. The whole time Lindsey and I were there, we were waiting and praying for her to find us, and she did! We started to cry and held on to her tightly and said,

"Don't leave us, Mommy!"

She stayed with us that night.

Dad reported Mom's absence to the leadership. They found Mom with us and started talking about her to the other followers and told them that she was not following God's will. Lindsey remembers that day and was very upset because they took us from Mom again. Lindsey was four years old and her job was washing the dirty cloth diapers. She remembers that the house was full of kids, and there was hardly any food to eat or adults to watch the kids, and it was very cold. One day, our mom told us she was planning on escaping with us as soon as the baby was born. We were to keep it a secret and not tell a soul.

Berg sent out a newsletter to the colonies and declared that everyone should go visit their birth parents. He said that in this test of faith the true followers would return back to him. All COG members, all over the world, took their children and left to visit their worldly families. My parents had to donate their old station wagon to the COG so we didn't have a car and took a bus to Ohio where my grandparents lived. When we arrived, my grandparents did not want to take us in. Fiona couldn't stand the thought of us living with them, and she sent us back on a Greyhound bus. Eight months pregnant, Mom cried almost the whole way back.

Berg had brainwashed all of the members to believe that their biological parents were just instruments used to birth them, and that our godly parents were the leaders in the COG! We were taught that our worldly families were our enemies, as the Bible said: "and a man's foes shall be those of his own house hold." We were taught to witness to our worldly families, and if they didn't forsake all or help us out financially, we were to turn our backs on them. Berg knew that most members' parents were not emotionally able to immediately take them back with open arms, and that most members would be sent away.

When my family arrived back to the commune in Woodland Park, Colorado, we discovered that many of the members were very sick, including my father. It was an outbreak of hepatitis. Something happened the day before Dad got sick. All the members were in the dining room waiting for lunch to be served.

My mom was in line with everyone else when the cook wearing an apron approached her and whispered in her ear-

"Selah".

He was warning her not to eat the stew and was risking getting into trouble. Selah was a special word that was used only in emergencies that meant *warning*. She looked at him with a serious expression and said-

"Why Selah, and why me?"

"Because it has raccoon in it and might not be safe to eat!"

The cook saw that Mom was pregnant and didn't want her to get sick.

She remembered his face; he was the young man who had burned his hand with hot grease, and she had helped him and prayed for him. After that meal many people—men, women, and children—acquired hepatitis. Several people lost their lives. We were told that God was "dealing with them and their families for their sins and disobedience. We were controlled by fear.

1972 Washington

After the deaths, the COG received a lot of negative publicity in Woodland Park. One young mom reportedly tried to leave with her daughter, and they were later discovered dead. Perhaps these were more fear tactics on the part of the COG leaders, but we'll never know the truth! The leadership decided it best to send our family to another colony in Burlington, Washington. This commune was huge. It had a large mess hall and a school for the kids which they called a kibbutz. A "real" kibbutz is a community in Israel based on agriculture farms. The COG used the term kibbutz to mean that the commune facility or colony had a separate area containing school supplies that was designated for schooling their children. Berg based his initial cult organization on his "interpretation of the kibbutz model"[9].

We were taken to the airport and boarded a flight to Seattle, Washington. We were greeted at the airport by COG "brethren" who took us to a camp called Global Missions Bible Camp in Burlington. The camp also had a free store. The store was very organized and well-managed. When new members joined and forsook all their belongings, their things would be placed in the free store. Worthy members were granted permission to get things they needed from the store for free. Any gifts that our relatives sent were first picked over by the leaders and then whatever was left was put in

---

[9]   A book titled "Cults and The Family by Lita Linzer Schwartz and Florence W. Kaslow

the free store. The leaders told everyone that it was God's commandment to forsake all and have faith that the Lord will provide.

That year, Fiona sent us a huge box of Christmas gifts, but the leaders told Mom that we were not worthy to have the toys, and they distributed the gifts among themselves. Later on, Mom found out that the leaders had distributed the toys between their own sons and daughters.

In late January 1972, Mom's water broke and she went into labor with her third baby. The midwife prepared the room in our cabin as a birthing room; she had expected that since our mom had already given birth to two children that she knew what to do. However, Lindsey and I were both born in hospitals and Mom was under medication and had never experienced natural childbirth. Mom was told to trust in God, have faith, and push the baby out. Mom was weak and unhealthy because she had not received nutritious food or vitamins during her pregnancy.

After hours of pushing and trying to give birth, she became very weak and sick with a fever. She was in a lot of pain; after twenty-four hours of labor, she still couldn't deliver the baby. The leaders and midwives had a meeting and decided that Mom was having difficulty because she did not have enough faith. They quoted to her, "according to her faith let it be done unto her" (MK 9:29 and MK 11:22). They put Mom and Dad in a truck and drove them to the nearest hospital, about a forty-five minute drive, and dropped them off at the emergency room.

The leaders knew Mom needed to go to the hospital, but they didn't like the idea of sending her to the hospital where she would be among outsiders and could be influenced by the systemites. Mom was rushed into the delivery room; the doctors were very concerned because they could not hear a heartbeat from the baby. Mom was given a saddle block, a large needle inserted into the spinal cord to numb her from the waist down. The doctor inserted forceps to pull the baby out; he expected that the baby had died in the womb. The doctor was shocked by the sound of a faint cry.

They immediately took Mom and the baby to intensive care. The doctor told Mom and Dad that if they had waited five minutes longer, both Emily and Mom would have surely died. The leaders instructed Dad that Mom and baby had to go back to the camp the following day. The doctors would not allow him to take Mom and Emily then, so they stayed another day. Mom said she never wanted to leave the hospital because all of the nurses and doctors treated her with love and kindness. Nevertheless, Dad took Mom and the baby back to the camp without the doctors' approval. When Mom got back, everyone was talking about her, and the leaders were not happy with her.

Dad had to go to another camp for training. After he returned and a few months had passed, things seemed to go back to normal. Mom had been confiding in Dad that she wanted to leave, and Dad told the leaders that Mom wanted to have a home of their own, that she wanted to live a normal life, have a stove of her own, and to put us in a real school. A few leaders called for Mom and explained that they had been praying about her and the Lord had revealed to them that she was possessed by a demon. They were going to perform an exorcism to cast the demon out. They spoke to Mom and Dad together and told her she needed to want to be saved and needed to want the demon to come out of her, or it wouldn't work.

They warned Mom that she could have convulsions, and all sorts of terrible things, so they would have to hold her down. Several men, including Dad held her down, and pinned her to the floor. They were screaming loudly, praying and shouting, "Rebuke the Devil in Jesus' holy name," over and over again. They told Mom she had to scream out and shout to force the demon out of her. Mom was crying hysterically and repeating after them, as they told her to. She said, "Please, God, save me and deliver me from evil." But nothing horrible happened. There was no foaming at the mouth, no convulsions, no rolling of the eyes, no vomiting. The worst thing that happened was that Mom was heartbroken and had suffered the emotional abuse of being held down and screamed at, plus she had bruises on her wrists and ankles.

The next day, two men named David and Jacob escorted Mom to the leaders' office to talk to her but also to have her sign over the monthly $50 check she received from gram. Every time mom received a letter and check from Gram, they would let her read the letter but forced her to sign over the check to them. Jacob also brought in Dad to listen in on the conversation and told Mom that they talked with Dad and it had been decided our family would be going to Seattle, Washington. Jacob said that God told them it would be a "better place" for her family (to mom it sounded like just another relocation).

Meanwhile, some of the women leaders went into Mom's cabin and took her Bible, coat, and the few personal items she had. They even took the baby's diapers and left only a few. They also left a box in the cabin.

When Mom got back to her cabin, she saw the box and thought it was a farewell gift and she was excited to open it. She opened the box and saw old, dirty, torn-up clothes. She looked around her cabin and noticed that they had taken her coat, Bible, and diapers. She was shocked and upset. Mom knew it was not right, but there was nothing she could do. The leadership knew how to control the members into believing that people who wanted to live differently from them were defying God's will.

All five of us got into a van with Jacob and another man and drove to Seattle. The van pulled up in front of an old brick house. It was cold and dreary. It was also completely empty and there was no electricity. There was one little bench inside the house and a wagon in the backyard. The kitchen had a small box of army surplus food and there were some old blankets on the floor. That was it!

The two men entered the house with us. As soon as we all stepped inside, Jacob looked at Mom and said-

"You and your three daughters are being excommunicated from the **COG**!"

He quoted this Bible verse by way of explanation: "As the mother is so are the daughters" (EZK 16:44)

"We decided your daughters are going to be unbelievers like you"

Mom suddenly realized this was their plan to leave her alone with her daughters.

"And Abraham rose up early in the morning, and took the bread, and a bottle of water, and gave it unto Hagar, putting it on her shoulder, and the child, and sent her away: and she departed, and wandered in the wilderness of Beersheba" (Genesis 21:14); Jacob quoted her.

Jacob told Mom that "the Lord was sending us out of the camp," but the Lord gave Dad a choice to remain with us or go back with them. Sebastian chose to go back with them. Mom cried hysterically and begged Dad on her hands and knees for forgiveness, and to stay with us and not leave, but he got back in the van with the men and left.

We were all alone in this strange, big, old empty house, and we curled up together on the floor and cried. We had no money, no electricity, no heat—just army surplus food. Mom found the wagon in the backyard and put us all into it, wrapped us up in the blankets that were left there, and prayed for God to lead us somewhere. She was not familiar with the area and had no idea where we were, but off we went in the wagon.

As Mom was pulling the wagon, we came upon a field with a pear tree. Mom thanked the Lord, picked some pears, and brought them back to the house. She cut them up and cooked them on the gas stove and added some syrup that was in the army surplus box. The next day we went for another ride in the wagon. Mom was pulling us in the wagon and she saw a small store. We walked by it and Mom saw that it was a building with a sandwich shop in front and an apartment towards the back. She walked a couple steps further and saw a truck in the back, several empty boxes and a dumpster. There was nobody around and there was no lid to the dumpster. She walked up to it and looked inside. There were two boxes thrown in the dumpster that had empty canned foods and also fresh food. There was half a loaf of bread, lettuce and tomatoes. There were two packages of donuts and apples. She was so relieved! She took most of the food that was in the boxes and we ate it for the next two days. She told us that the Lord had put that food there for us!

Elizabeth pulling the wagon with Lindsey, Sophia and baby Emily

The next day, we went for another ride in the wagon. It was very cold and it started to snow. Mom began crying, as our situation was growing worse because of the lack of heat and electricity in our house. As she was pulling us along, a car drove by and slowed down, and Mom got scared, but there was nowhere to go, not even a store in sight. The car turned around and drove by slowly again, and a window rolled down and a woman's voice said

"Hi there, are you all right? Where are you going?"

Mom was crying, and said, "I don't know! I don't know where to go, or what to do."

The lady driving asked, "Where do you live? Do you want us to take you home?

Mom said "We don't have a home."

The two ladies, who introduced themselves as Annette and Linda, pulled over and offered to help get us out of the cold. Linda said that she had just made a big pot of soup and their house was close by; she could get together some warm clothes for us and feed us some hot, homemade vegetable soup and corn bread.

We all four got into their car and left the wagon on the sidewalk. When we got to their home, they gave us towels to dry off, clean, dry clothes, and big bowls of homemade vegetable soup. We stayed with Annette and Linda for several days and never went back to that vacant house. Later, we found out that the old brick house had been a vacant COG "widow's colony", a home just for single moms and their children. "For example, in 1971 a "widow's colony" was set up in Knoxville, Tennessee, where mothers without husbands shared childcare and expenses[10]. Mothers and children that lived in the widow's colonies were considered to be lower

---

[10] A book called "The Children of God; A Make-Believe Revolution?" written by Author Ruth Wangerin.

level members. It was not a place where high leader associate women and children would live, they were given much better resources and help.

Mom explained to Annette and Linda that Dad had left us and that we had been evicted from our home. She never spoke of the COG to them, and how awful her situation was and how she had been excommunicated and abandoned by them. She had been so brainwashed that she thought that perhaps the COG had been right about her, that she was a sinner with no faith. Annette and Linda took us to a welfare office and they came in with all of us and waited there until we received assistance. We lived with them until we received a check in the mail, at which time they helped us find a little house and moved us in. Little by little people started coming by and dropping off food, clothes, blankets, and even furniture. We bought another wagon from a thrift shop and would walk to the grocery store and stock up on food.

CHAPTER 5

Dad Returns and Mom Rejoins the Cult

A nearby church donated a sewing machine for Mom, and she began to earn money by sewing for other people. She would do anything from alterations to making clothes, even fancy dresses. Mom was doing well but she was lonely and missed Dad. She got in touch with him and he came to visit. They got back together and he moved in with us.

Dad said the Lord told the leaders that he was supposed to get back together with Mom and that we were going to move to Texas to another colony. Although Mom didn't want to go back and live in a commune again with the COG, she didn't want us to grow up without our dad and she wanted to stay with him.

Mom became pregnant with our first baby brother. We got a "drive-away car" and left Seattle. A drive-away-car is similar to an auto rental service in the sense that a car is provided for you to use to transport you from one location to another as opposed to taking a bus or other means of transportation. Dad agreed to make a detour to visit our Gram in Long Beach, California before we headed to El Paso, Texas. Gram had a cozy home and we were happy and comfortable there. Gram's little place was very organized and cute. She and I got close to each other right away—our birthdays were close together and I thought that was special. While we (Mom, Dad, Lindsey, Emily and I) stayed there, we all had chores and helped out daily. I liked to wash dishes after dinner and help keep her place as perfect as it was when we arrived. Gram would throw a blanket on the living room floor, put all of us on it, and bring us yummy sandwiches, chips and Kool-Aid while we watched TV.

In Gram's tiny kitchen, all the cups and plates had a special place. Everything in her house had its place, yet she somehow made room for all five of us. It was very different from life with the cult. Gram was so sweet to us, and our life with her was calm and loving. My sisters and I were allowed to watch *Little House on the Prairie* every night, whereas in the cult, children were not allowed to watch any television. We could only watch biblical movies like *The Ten Commandments* and *Jesus Christ Superstar*.

1973 Texas

For a little while, Mom had managed to escape COG. But now that Dad was back in the picture and Mom pregnant again, we ended up doing what he wanted to do. We moved to a colony in El Paso. Mom was given a lot of responsibility in this new COG colony. Shortly after we got settled in El Paso, we were told we were being transferred to Laredo, Texas. Off we went to another COG colony in Laredo, which was a border town.

There was a lot going on, but Dad had his plan. He was determined to take us to the mission field in Mexico. While we were living in a multi-family home with the cult, my first brother **Andretti** was born in the fall of 1973. Mom took better care of herself during this pregnancy and Andretti was a very healthy baby. He was my birthday present since he was born one day after mine. We always understood each other when we were together. We didn't have to say too much about what we were doing or what we needed because it felt like we were united.

When Andretti was a baby and started talking, he had trouble saying Lindsey and called her "Lini," which became her nickname. Later the other babies called her Lini too. We started a nickname trend: whatever our new babies called us became our cute, little nicknames. Andretti was always singing, he was a hyper baby and he grew to become a very creative boy.

1973 Mexico

In 1973 when I was five years old we were a family of six. My parents had no outside source of income, but Dad said that the Lord had showed him that we were supposed to go to Mexico. This was going to be our test of faith as a family. I was so excited, and we all talked about how happy we were about going to Mexico to be real missionaries.

The COG provided us with an old, green school bus, which we converted to a motor home by building little bunk beds for Lindsey, Emily, Andretti and me. Mom and Dad slept on a small foam rubber mattress on the floor. Mom made little curtains (again) for the windows, and we called it home!

I was five and we were on our own, starting our missionary work in Mexico. Even though we were part of this horrible cult we were sincere about believing in God and we were serious about our missionary outreach. We packed the green bus full of boxes of used clothing and food to give to the poor. It was an amazing experience. We would go to different organizations and explain our mission and ask if they wanted to help us in our efforts by donating clothes and food. We were overjoyed to be going into villages and distributing free clothes and groceries.

Our past is complicated with good and bad. We have a negative aspect of our life as it relates to the cult. But we also have amazing memories from the people we went to visit and our missionary work in Mexico. I remember reaching out and touching the hearts of people that were suffering. I was a happy child and I could see that some of these people we visited needed to hear about how wonderful God was and how much they are loved.

Based on many studies conducted about the COG (**present day**), obviously back then some of the cult adult members were not doing things for the right reasons but I'm sure some of them really thought they were. As for my family we loved reaching out to other people and got caught up in the interaction and magic of sharing our time and life with people that lived in poverty stricken villages.

1973, Back to Texas

Very shortly after that, we were involved in an accident, and the Mexican authorities confiscated the bus. We had to return to the U.S. Mom's dad, my grandpa, lived in San Antonio. We were desperate for help, and Grandpa was a Christian and probably didn't really understand what we were involved in but wanted to help us. He offered to help us out if we moved there, so we moved to San Antonio and Grandpa helped pay for a one-room efficiency apartment. It had a couch that pulled out into a bed, one bathroom with a real bathtub, and a teeny tiny kitchen with a tiny sink and tiny stove and refrigerator. It was our new home.

Now we were not living under the roof of the COG, so that meant we had no help or support from them either. My parents had been strongly influenced by the cult. They were struggling with knowing what God wanted us to do, knowing what the cult said we should do and knowing what they needed to do for their family. We continued to witness (litness) and receive donations as a way of making money. Dad sent Mom, who was pregnant with baby number five and the kids out to litness while he stayed with the babies. He said we received more donations than he did, and we believed we were real missionaries.

So many things were going through my parents' mind that it must have been really hard for them to make sense out of their life. They were young and naïve and knew some of the admired COG leaders started out like they did. They had been told that dedicated believers were rewarded and blessed beyond imagination.

Our apartment home felt good, and we were all excited about our new life. It had not been too long since we had stayed with our sweet Gram, and I think that experience made it easier for us to want a better life and be away from the cult's rules. Months earlier when we stayed with Grams she gave us lots of fun love and stability in our daily routines. I guess Lindsey and I never really had that before. For once we could be just normal kids, hang out, watch TV, consume yummy junk food and perform light house work. Basically we experienced a healthy *childhood*. There was the absence of us feeling like our existence was all about owing something to someone or on edge about not knowing what our next responsibility would be and which person would be benefiting from our duties that we had to perform.

Our parents loved music but the COG did not permit its followers to listen to worldly music. Gradually they started playing non-cult music. Some of their favorites were Cat Stevens, James Taylor, America Crosby Stills Nash and Young, Simon and Garfunkel, and Carole King. It was so nice listening to their music, I didn't think about it much back then, but it was professional music and sounded better than what we were used to hearing.

We were excited about living together like this, with our *own* family. But because of all the brainwashing we had endured even though we were happy we still felt like something was missing and we were doing something wrong. What we really needed at that point (but did not get) was some serious therapy and deprogramming. The brainwashing included ingraining in us that going to public schools, having regular jobs, watching television, and going to church was interacting with the worldly society, and was wrong in God's eyes.

CHAPTER 6

Moving to Mexico

1974-1976 Mexico (Monterey, Queretaro, Mexico City, Acapulco)

Our quiet safe life didn't last long. Dad decided it was time for us to go back to the mission field in Mexico and once again we were in full force living amongst the COG cult. We were submerged in their environment, the people, the music and all the rituals and rules.

We started to learn Spanish before we went back to Mexico. When I first started to study and learn it I became confident about learning a foreign language and it was exciting and fun. We began speaking with the tapes every day. I played the tapes and repeated the words in Spanish. Cat, gato; house, casa; street, calle.

We moved to Mexico and started traveling a lot from town to town (with just Mom, Dad and us kids). We stayed in Monterey, Saltillo, Queretaro, Mexico City, Puebla, Cuernavaca, Acapulco, and went back and forth between Mexico and Laredo. We had now been living the COG life for over four years.

1976 Pueblo, Mexico

We moved to Pueblo, Mexico where **Luigio** was born in July 1975. Luigio had two nicknames. We called him "Lui" when he was first born, but once we saw his angelic personality, we started to call him "Angelito." When mom went into labor with Luigio, she and Dad had to take a taxi to look for a midwife to help her with the delivery. The midwife gave Mom cinnamon tea, which helped her with the labor. Luigio was born naturally at home and the delivery was great. He was a healthy, beautiful baby boy.

Emily was real close to Luigio. He called her "Emi" when he started talking and that became her nickname. He was a quiet baby, and as a toddler he had the cutest round face, big blue eyes, and the darkest hair of us all. When you looked at him, he looked back at you with the sweetest smile.

Of course now I realize that being a member of a *Christian* Cult is a bad thing but I also know that when I pray I feel like I'm praying to the same God that I was back then. Hearing about all the things the COG has done to children and families and knowing firsthand how the children are treated (deceived and abused in many ways) is a permanent painful dark side of our past. So that explains why for years I just didn't know how to make sense of it all.

Nevertheless, when I closed my eyes to pray a vision of a kind gentle man looking a little like a grey bearded wise elderly man appeared in my mind and I felt peace.

Present day, when I pray I immediately connect with him (that same vision) and don't expect him to fix my problems but I ask him to watch over whatever issue I am dealing with and I thank him for all his blessings (my family, my job and our health). When I finish praying I still have a special peace that comes over me just like I did when I was a little girl.

We knew some Mexican Christians (non-cult people) who wanted to help support our missionary work. A local businessman donated a canvas tent, which was about ten by twelve feet and certainly big enough for all of us. We loved that tent because it was our own small new home. We kept it clean and there was enough room for Mom, Dad, Lindsey, Emily, Andretti, Luigio and me.

When we were living at campgrounds we could use the toilets, take hot showers, and we could use an extension cord to cook hot meals on our electric skillet. Mom would set up her sewing machine outside on the picnic tables and sew and mend our clothes. She also made all of us our own backpacks!

Typical day for the Santino at the camp ground, Sebastian playing the guitar, Elizabeth sewing and children playing

My parents now pioneered a COG colony in Mexico. As time went on, this colony household included more families and everyone followed a regular schedule. Each day, the adults set up long tables and gathered around holding hands, prayed, and ate dinner together at the exact same time every day. I used to think to myself,

"Gosh, how on earth do the adults know when to stop cooking dinner so we can eat at the same time everyday?"

I was seven years old now and very impressed with their organizational skills.

We all looked forward to our fellowship with everyone at night, and, of course, we couldn't wait to sing and dance. By now Mom and Dad were really good and knew most of the songs. Not all the other families were musically inclined, so my parents started to lead the singing and Dad played new songs for everyone. We were so proud when he sang his solos and saw how everyone listened and loved his voice.

All the mothers that had been members for a while were given special authority and special jobs within the large household. Their husbands were also identified as up-and-coming leaders in the group. I was so proud of my mother's job and the fact that all the kids liked her. I used to watch her while she worked; thinking how all the other kids probably wished their mothers were as funny and nice as mine and had a respectful important job.

Mom's job was to work with young moms and children. One of her duties was to teach the children how to conserve resources in everything they did. She taught us that if we learned how to conserve for Jesus, then we would receive more blessings. Mom would gather all the children together and take us around from room to room, showing us the proper way to take care of every part of the house. For example, she crowded all of us into the bathroom and taught us that we could conserve resources by using only two sheets of toilet paper for number one and three sheets for number two.

She was very expressive and wanted to make sure we all understood, so she showed us by example. She said,

"Now, children, this is what you *have* been doing when you go number one."

She made a silly expression and pulled out almost half a roll of toilet paper and wrapped it all around her fist. The kids all giggled. She had a glob of toilet paper wrapped around her hand.

"Now, this is wasteful," she took the toilet paper off her hand, and with a sweet smile said,

"Now this is what you *should* do."

With great sophistication, she very delicately unrolled exactly two sheets of toilet paper. All the kids laughed again.

"Waste not, want not," and "that which is willfully wasted shall be willfully wanted." It stuck with us.

My brothers, sisters and I prayed about everything. Since we believed that the Lord was providing for us and everything that happened was God's will, we always asked him to help us with what we wanted. The more time you spent praying and begging the Lord, the better chance your prayers would be answered. Some adults would even start crying and freaking out when they prayed. Prayer time was taken very seriously.

She taught us about love, respect and to get along and take care of each other. We had to be fair to each other so that nobody felt left out or got their feelings hurt. So to give you an example, if I wanted to play with my friend I knew I had to invite my older sister and my younger sister and then I would ask Mom if we all could go play. Even though a kid might ask one of us to play with them usually the other brothers and sisters would tag along.

We had a large family and very few toys, but we were happy and stayed busy. Mom tickled us, chased us around, and played games with us. Dad was also a lot of fun, especially when he would do headstands for a long time on the floor and he wouldn't drop his legs down until his face turned purple. But most of all, it was really amazing how he could walk all around the floor upside down on his hands. We never saw anyone else do that and it looked so funny, like an upside down magician man.

When my brother Andretti was about three and I was eight, our mother would send me out daily to hunt him down. Andretti was a terror to say the least, and bringing him home usually took about an hour. I had it all figured out: first I would find him, sweet talk him, and play with him for a while. Then I would ask him if he was hungry, and if that did not work I would start running real fast, chasing him all over the yard. Finally, when I caught him, he would bite, kick, scream, and pull my hair. Sometimes this process took longer, and it became harder to chase him as it got darker. I did not want this to be my job anymore and when I told Mom she said-

"Honey, I know it is not easy, but you are so good with Andretti, and there really isn't anyone else that can catch him."

Sometimes while I was "on the job" hunting down little Andretti, I would take advantage of the situation and stop by the Mexican neighbors' houses and watch TV for a few minutes through their front door. In Mexico the families would all crowd together in the late afternoons. Their tiny living rooms were often packed with people and they always left the front door open. I would start out by saying hello and standing outside their front door. From the intense look on my face, I guess they could tell I was very interested in the show, so they would tell me to come in, make myself comfortable, and stay for as long as I liked.

I felt guilty about this because I was supposed to be finding my little brother, but I could not pull myself away. After a while, the neighbors looked forward to my visits and were eager to talk to me. My Spanish was good and they had all kinds of questions they wanted to ask me. Most of their questions were about the United States and I really did not know what to tell them. I didn't know much about the U.S. because I was so young when I lived there, and all I really wanted to do was watch their television.

Since Lindsey, Emily and I were not in school, my parents would take us to campsites all the time, and we would stay there for days when we were traveling. We all knew how to help roll out the tent and take it back down. The best part about camping was picking the weeping willow tree branches, braiding them, and putting them in our hair. We chased each other around and played hide and go seek. I didn't like the flying bugs that I heard all night long, and I didn't like it when it was my turn to take those cold baths with the hose, Mom called them "navy baths".

To be honest there were a lot of other little things that irritated me about camping. Inside the tent I always wished the ground was flat (I hated all those little bumps and rocks), that would have made it feel more like a house. And, I hated the dirt that would always get inside the tent. We had a little broom and swept the inside of the tent every day. Also, I just didn't like how anything could get inside the tent, there were always bugs. The good things were the camp fires, the beautiful trees and all the space we had to play outside. We looked forward to the meals Mom cooked us with her trusty, electric skillet. She took it with her everywhere. She would plug it in and invent a new meal every day.

We moved and started traveling all over Mexico and living in our car again. During this time we didn't have our tent (for some reason), so at night Mom tied a knot in the end of a sheet, placed it over the car door, and closed the door with the knot outside. Then she did the same on the other side. When the car doors were closed, the sheets formed little hammocks. She did that for the back seats also and it made 2 sleeping hammocks. We would sleep two of the biggest kids in the car seats, two of the smaller kids would sleep in the hammocks, and Mom and Dad would sleep in the back.

Santino Babies sleeping in custom made car hammocks

Of course we barely had any money, so we were always worried about how we were going to eat or get money for gasoline. But to us, or at least to us kids, even though we were worried about it, things like "money" or "gas" were just things that people needed. We didn't realize that out of the huge list of all the things that people needed, those were very big ones. We were also accustomed to picking up and being on the go and that is what we had to do when we needed to figure out how to get food or raise money.

Traveling for us was hard work because we were always unloading and reloading, especially when we lived in our car. Mostly to me because I could not stand for the station wagon to be messy and disorganized and it seemed like right after I straightened everything up it would just get messy again, it was very frustrating. Although our life was unpredictable and unstable, we still had fun times and got excited about being somewhere different when we traveled. When we arrived in the new towns at night, Dad would always wake me up because he knew how much I loved looking at the towns all lit up.

It was obvious to me that our lifestyle was not like everyone else's. We were taught that we should save as many people per day as possible because Jesus was returning any minute, and the unsaved people would go straight to hell unless they were saved in time. From my experience as a child, this was something that I thought about all the time. Most days I thought to myself, *this is probably the last day before Jesus comes*". When it was my turn to go out to litness, I tried really hard to talk to strangers and save as many people as I could. But I also wanted to finish my work so I could have fun in the town. Almost nightly my dad would read us the Bible and give us a couple new verses to memorize. We would talk about a Bible verse and how we could apply it to what we were going to do the next day.

It was hard explaining to adults and other kids why I didn't go to school and why my parents and other adults with us did not go to work every day. I tried to explain and said something like, "Our family was chosen by God to preach his word and save people so they could go to heaven." But what I was saying began to sound strange to me. I felt like all my friends that lived nearby us were also good people even though they weren't like us.

We had activities in our life that were fun and we made the most out our living conditions but in many cases we were simply innocent victims. No doubt we cherish our happy memories but it doesn't change the bad experiences we endured as a result of being members of the COG.

Some of our good memories are genuinely wonderful experiences and others I suspect were merely cover-ups for the unjust core of how the COG lived and the things they engaged in as part of their daily activities.

I knew that our neighbor friends were learning how to be smart in school and that they had nice houses, cars, and other things because their parents worked every day. I didn't believe that they were sinners because they did not believe what we believed. Sometimes when we traveled, we would stay in people's homes who were not part of the COG. They would take all of us in, serve us café con leche y pan dulce[11]. They were always very hospitable and helped us, and yet we were taught to be against the way they lived.

We had lived in Mexico for years now and embraced the culture; rich language, food and traditions, it became a big part of what we enjoyed in life. There were a few cultural things we loved such as watching Mexican traditional performers and going to festivals, and they were all free!

---

[11]   Pan Dulces are little loaves of bread made without preservative. They have sugar sprinkled on top and are served in Mexico with breakfast or as a dessert.

While our family spent good times together going into town or visiting small villages we; watched Mariachi[12] performers and admired the Mexican Dancers, one of the best was the *Conchero* dancers[13]

We loved all the popular foods in Mexico. Cajeta[14] is one of them; it is very thick and rich and looks like caramel. It was a real treat to spread cajeta on your bread or fruit, it was a special food that could be found in most Mexican homes. Rompope[15] is a delicious popular eggnog type of drink that is made with rum. We loved to drink it in Mexico when it was served at special celebrations and parties. Since it had rum as a main ingredient I'm not sure why we were allowed to drink it occasionally (either it was because we were under poor supervision at the time or maybe because it had nutritional ingredients we needed in our diet like eggs and milk—who knows).

---

[12] Mariachi goes beyond music, it is the sum of a cultural revolution expressed through a group of musicians, dressed in popular clothing (most recently charro suits) which encompasses the essence of Mexico and its people. It is something cultural, spiritual and traditional that is unique to this country, an experience not to be missed. From MexConnect by Camille Collins. "Mariachi bands are a symbol of Mexico. Mariachis date from the time in the 1860s that the French army occupied Mexico. Many French soldiers married Mexican women, and they hired small bands to play at their weddings." And "later called mariachis, from the French word for marriage (marriage).", from The Lands, Peoples, and Cultures Series Created by Bobbie Kalman.

[13] Dance is an important part of Mexican culture. Mexicans feel that it keeps them in touch with their native heritage. *Conchero* dancers often perform at Mexican celebrations called fiestas. Men and women dance ancient native dances to the music of a guitar or lute. Their colorful costumes include tall, plumed headdresses, wide capes, sequined robes, embroidered shields, and clusters of bells and dried shells at the ankles." They "traveled from fiesta to fiesta, dancing for hours, from The Lands, Peoples, and Cultures Series Created by Bobbie Kalman.

[14] Cajeta is a delicious Mexican sweet made from goat or cow's milk made into a thick syrup.

[15] Rompope is a traditional Mexican version of eggnog that locals either make at home or purchase all year long. The original rompope drink came from Puebla Mexico in the 17th century.

We all had to take doses of Cod Liver Oil[16] in Mexico as a nutritional supplement that helped support the immune system. I remember whenever it was available to us the adults would line up all the kids outside and force every single one of us to drink a "full" tablespoon. We always knew that we would have to drink it every day until we were completely out of the Cod Liver Oil bottle. Even though they explained to us that it was extremely nutritional and our growing bodies needed it, we still always complained about taking it. Of course there were always some kids that would get spankings because they refused to drink it. I can't remember if I ever refused it but I know Lindsey did, she was stubborn and had strong will.

I don't know if it taste any better now in the 21st century but back then it was just about the worst tasting thing I ever drank. I remember sometimes the adults had both types; the clear one and the creamy one, and they asked us which one we wanted but it didn't matter because they both had a disgusting taste.

When we were doing our missionary work, we visited nursing homes and impoverished villages in Mexico. Before we left on these trips, we would all fill up our backpacks and be prepared to spend the whole day out. We would leave early in the morning, and once we arrived at our mission site everything else about our lives just stopped. We poured out our hearts to these people; we put ourselves in their world. This means that we would sit with someone and talk to them and when they would start telling us about all their problems and crying to us we would say something to make them feel good and give them hope. It made them feel better and also made us feel good.

Mom had made gift packages to hand out, like combs and brushes, toothbrushes and toothpaste, deodorant and a little bottle of perfume,

---

[16]   During the Second World War, Cod Liver Oil Liquid was produced by the Company for the Ministry of Food under a free distribution scheme, the Welfare Food programme. This was therefore the biggest sampling/endorsement support for any healthcare product in history. In the 1970s it suddenly moved to the cutting edge of nutritional science. Provided by Seven Seas; a Merck Company.

shaving cream and scarves. As a young girl, Mom was a Brownie and a Girl Scout, and every year her troop would visit orphanages and take gifts. They made gift packages with mirrors, cookies, and toys. This is where she got the gift idea for our own missions.

In the nursing homes we connected with the people who lived there; they were so lonely. We were like waves of loving energy that swept them off their feet. Full of smiley faces, we performed musicals and skits for them in Spanish. They laughed and enjoyed the shows. They knew they were special to us. At the end of the day, we all knew we had made a difference, and we left feeling glad that we had done our best. Even still, we walked away with a sense of sadness knowing that their lives would continue to be lonely and that they would not be getting the care they needed.

When we visited the poverty villages, we would join in with the piñata birthday parties and whatever activities were going on at the time. The locals would welcome us and we would just hang out with them and have fun all day. Being around all those hungry, poor, and barely dressed children made us feel like we had so many blessings.

My parents also started a prison ministry. We were a little scared but excited, and we practiced our songs and prepared for it. We were told this was the type of work that Jesus did and we were doing something special to help these people. We arrived at the prison and went through security. We brought in food and sang several songs to the prisoners, sat with them, and witnessed to them. Lindsey remembers being so happy about praying with one of the prisoners; he had asked Jesus to come into his heart. She also felt like we were lucky to have a dad that wasn't in prison. A lot of the prison men we met had families and children that they never got to see.

**Santino Family on mission in a Mexican village,
Elizabeth is visiting a village home**

The early to mid 1970s followed two decades of epic Old Testament movies such as *Sodom and Gomorrah, The Ten Commandments, David and Goliath, Esther and the King* and several more.

We watched all of them.

These movies had massive battles, sword fights, natural disasters, and unbelievable miracles as was common in the Old Testament. The cult would use them to further brainwash its members.

The combination of sex, violence and drama in these Biblical stories fit many of their mind molding techniques.

The irony is that these movies showed immorality as being forbidden, such as Delilah's temptation of Samson while the Children of God cult members lived lives which actively practiced many of the same behaviors.

We studied the story about the Passover in the Bible and watched the movie. In this story Moses told the Pharaoh if the Egyptians didn't show they believed in God by putting lamb's blood on their front door, then they would be punished and their firstborn son would die.

"For the Jewish people Passover celebrated God's love for them. On the night of the first Passover when the Israelites were slaves in Egypt each Jewish family had painted the door of their home with lambs blood then they had gone inside, roasted the meat and eaten it. God had told them to do these things for two reasons. First, when he sent his angel to destroy the evil Egyptians the angel had been instructed to pass over any house with blood on the door. Second, God wanted to make sure that his people had something to eat before they left Egypt" (Exodus 12).

When Passover came, every home that was not marked with lamb's blood, the firstborn son died. In the movie we saw mothers holding their dead sons on their knees, screaming. I can hardly bear to think of it even now. Most of the movies we got to watch were like that, but this was one of the saddest and scariest for us and left a strong impression on me. Mom argued with Dad and didn't want us to watch the scary parts, but Dad said it would only make us stronger.

We studied the story of Abraham in the Bible and had watched the movie many times before. God commanded Abraham to take his son to the mountains to sacrifice him. Abraham was angry at God and said he wouldn't do it, but God told him that he had to. Abraham took his beloved son to the mountains. He built a sacrifice table and kissed and held his son tight. He laid his son on the table and tied him up with rope. He took out his knife and raised it high above his son. He said a prayer to God, and just before he started to lower the knife into his son's chest, God spoke to him. God said, "Abraham, stop. You do not have to sacrifice your son; you have proved your faith to me." And Abraham lowered his arms, untied his son, and they wept. Just then they saw that God had provided a lamb for them to sacrifice instead. We were taught that we had to be willing to sacrifice everything, even our children, if God commanded to do so.

CHAPTER 7

Dad Becomes Estranged from Us

1976 Saltillo, Mexico

In 1976 we moved to Saltillo, Mexico where **Sebastian Jr.** was born in March 1977. When we first moved there, we lived in our tent, but eventually we moved into a small house in a little village. From time to time people passing by would stay with us. Through the years, Mom and Dad had a lot of problems in their marriage.

Dad was traveling a lot and Mom started to go into labor with Sebastian Junior. Dad was out of town but made it home just before Sebastian Jr. was born. Dad didn't stick around and left again the next day. Mom was sure he had a girlfriend somewhere and said, just as dad was leaving,

"But we didn't decide on a name for him."

Dad said, "You name him."

Mom was worried because she did not want Dad to get mad at her for choosing a name he didn't like. Mom decided to name the baby after him so that he couldn't get mad.

Andretti was a big brother now. When Sebastian Jr. started talking he had trouble saying Andretti so he started calling him "Detti," so this became his nickname and it was easy for our new baby brothers to say. He was just as adorable as Luigio except he had very blonde hair and it was curly.

My dad became more and more set on traveling independently and doing his own thing. I guess he was serving his cult because he wasn't going to work every day to take care of us. Dad loved his children and missed us when he was gone, but he also wanted to follow the leadership and be successful with the COG. He became accustomed to having his freedom and had many relationships with other woman. There were many other wives like Mom who would stay home with the children waiting to hear back from their husbands that were constantly traveling. The cult brainwashed their members to the point that they had to keep believing—it was all they had in life. To the followers, it seemed like the leaders were speaking straight from the Bible. But really they would quote verses and use them to back up whatever it was that they were trying to control or make the members believe.

Most media accounts of the Children of God cult are accurate:

> "The Children of God (COG), later known as the Family of Love, the Family, and now the Family International (TFI), is a Christian religious group, widely referred to as a cult by the media, many in academia, and some former members, that started in 1968 in Huntington Beach, California, United States. It was an off shoot of the Jesus movement of the late 1960s, with many of its early converts drawn from the hippie movement. It was among the movements prompting the cult controversy of the 1970s and 1980s in the United States and Europe and triggered the first organized anti-cult group (FREEGOC)." "Don't be fooled by this one. They've adopted a more clean-cut appearance. They even performed in the white house in 1992." "C.O.G. appealed to the hippie generation with its message of "free" love and singing all in the name of Jesus. They are called the original Jesus "freaks"."[17]

---

[17]   From www.jesus-is-savior.com.

"Most contemporary debates about the applicability of "brainwashing" as a social scientific concept involve arguments over what (if any) utility it has when discussing conversion to some high-demand, alternative religions. Some sociologists of religion use the term "brainwashing" to apply to extreme social influences. Others restrict use of the term to situations involving forcible confinement and physical coercion, presumably amidst a group-indoctrination process. Since few such conversion situations exist, these sociologists avoid utilizing brainwashing within social scientific discourse. What they have overlooked, however, is the conceptual utility of the brainwashing concept, even with their restrictive definition, for analyzing some groups' efforts at retaining or reconverting members. This study examines an example of a brainwashing program—the camps and programs that the Children of God\The Family developed for its teen members. These programs included intense re-education programs in the context of physical, psychological, and socio-emotional punishments, often in confined or guarded camps. As a social scientific concept, "brainwashing" has explanatory usefulness for understanding The Family's harsh efforts both to increase the intensity of teens' commitment to the organization, and to foster compliance to leadership."

-Stephen A. Kent, Ph.D. and Deana Hall, M.A.[18]

They would attempt to back up their actions with the Bible. Some believed in extramarital relationships, specifically in sharing wives with other men. This was called "One Wife." The male leaders would go to their wives and quote them a verse in the Bible about unconditional love, and it became a free ticket for the leaders to sleep with another woman of their choice. And the women that wanted to did the same. It makes me sick and thank

---

[18] Published in CULTIC STUDIES JOURNAL Volume 17 (2000): 56-78., Brainwashing and Re-Indoctrination Programs in the Children of God/The Family. Stephen A. Kent, PhD. And Deana Hall, M.A., University of Alberta

God that I was not old enough to have any part in it! There have been many books written about the COG cult; several celebrities who were members in their childhood or young adulthood have spoken about their experiences.

The leaders used short pamphlets as visual aids in teaching their followers. These pamphlets were composed of text and explicit illustrations of men and women in sexual positions. Bible verses accompanied each picture. There was also additional text that reinterpreted the verse according to what the leader wanted us to believe. It was all part of the leadership's strategy of manipulation. We would also take the pamphlets with us to offer to people, passing them out on the streets and asking for donations for God.

As I mentioned, we believed that the sinners needed to be saved and it was our first priority to save as many people as we could because the end-time was coming. We all had backpacks fully supplied with powdered eggs, dried fruits packaged in foil, lanterns, sleeping bags, and other survival necessities. Everyone in the "family" was required to have one of these backpacks in order to be prepared when Jesus returned. As a way of demonstration the COG would have the members watch *Sound of Music*. I watched it so many times that I felt like my family was an extension of the family in *Sound of Music*. I connected with the movie so much that I didn't know what was real. Our instructions from the COG were to prepare to leave for the mountains just like the family did in *The Sound of Music*.

We were supposed to be ready to grab our backpacks, leave everything else behind, and flee to the mountains. When we had emergencies and had to eat our survival food, we were always in a hurry to refill it.

I remember asking Dad all the time,

"When is Jesus coming? Is it time yet?"

I could not believe that all this time had passed and he still wasn't here. My dad would look at me and say,

"We won't know until the last minute, which is why we have to always be ready."

The last time I asked my Dad about this, I was older and starting to want to have boyfriends and grow up to become a woman. So I asked my Dad again,

"When is Jesus coming?"

He did not answer. I got tears in my eyes and said,

"I'll never be able to grow up if Jesus returns, will I, Dad?"

I was worried about my life and it bothered me that I didn't know if I would become a woman or not. My dad answered and said,

"Well, honey, I can't really give you an answer." At the time I thought he just felt bad for me because he got to grow up and knew I never would.

One time Mom and Dad had a little money and wanted to get the kids some new toys, but it had to be something practical. They went to the store and bought groceries and picked out some very special little play sets. They bought several broom, bucket, and mop sets for the kids to play with. When they got home, there was a neighbor changing his motor oil outside. Mom and Dad left the toys outside and Mom went in to fix dinner. She called all of us in the house to eat and saw that one of the mops was sitting inside a large bucket full of motor oil. She was very upset and right away lined all the kids up to question them.

She asked Andretti firmly,

"Andretti, did you put that mop in that bucket?"

He shook his head and said no. Still upset, she turned to Sebastian and asked,

"Sebastian, did you put that mop in that bucket of oil?"

He shook his head and said no. She turned to Luigio and asked,

"Luigio, did you put that mop in that bucket of oil?"

He looked at her with scared, darling toddler eyes and said

"I not Luigio."

Mom just couldn't be upset any more, it was so cute. He had melted her heart!

We had so much fun together as a family. We often made candy popcorn balls and homemade pizza. Lindsey, Emily, and I cooked with Mom because it was really fun for us. I asked my mother to roll my hair every night so I could look beautiful in the morning. She would take a white sheet and tear it into long rags. She took each thin strip of rag and tied a knot around each piece of my hair, then she rolled the pieces all the way to my scalp and tied another knot to keep it in place. Later I started doing it myself and it didn't take me very long. Lindsey also curled her hair with rags, but she already had wavy hair and didn't need to do it every night. In the morning, Mom would take out all the rolled-up rags and help me fix my hair. Of course, after that, my little sister wanted Mom to curl her hair too, and we would all go to bed with rag doll curls in our hair.

> *"To be in your children's memories tomorrow, you have to be in their lives today."—Anonymous*

I remember being so excited to wake up every morning and get ready to walk several blocks down to the tortillaría. In Mexican villages there were many little shacks in the middle of the street, some with a tortilla machine inside and several people working. People would line up early every morning to get delicious, fresh corn tortillas. One time, I took a tortilla out of the wrapped package and started eating it. One of the leaders yelled at me and told me I had no right to eat that without permission. Mom got mad at him, and told me,

"Honey, go ahead and eat it." She looked at the leader with a stern face and quoted from the Bible, "Muzzle not the ox that treadeth out the corn!"

We did not celebrate Christmas with a tree and presents. It was a special occasion for us, though, and we all gathered together in the living room to celebrate the birth of Christ. We had communion on Christmas Day and usually had a nice dinner.

Another aspect of the COG indoctrination was something they called "flirty fishing." It was a horrible practice the leader came up with and it destroyed many families.

Berg prophesied that the female members in the COG were ordained by God to go flirty fishing and share their bodies sexually to prove God's love.

Of course, this was one man's sick and perverted way of bringing in large amounts of money to support his cult. Mo even wrote a letter called "Hookers for Jesus!" Women of all ages were required to literally "lay down" their lives for the love of God! They went out and flirty fished, partied, drank wine with the "worldly and ungodly," and received payment as prostitutes.

The leadership categorized the members by their faith and usually whatever the leadership thought the member could handle. Mom quoted the leaders as preaching "Babes (women) are to be given sweet milk, while stronger members are to receive the strong meat of the word". It again illustrates how the cult combined explicit sexual practices with Biblical teachings.

The Mo letters, which were his direct communications to the cult were categorized by: leaders only, disciples only, friends and families only, and associate members only.

As associate members, we were no longer required to live with the full-time members and also we were not allowed to read all of their Mo letters. What was required of disciples was not required of associate members.

Dad developed our own eight-person family band. He started scheduling gigs all over Mexico. Mom sewed us matching costumes. She made the boys blue velvet jump suits with white satin shirts, and she made us girls red velvet skirts with white satin blouses. We loved to wear our costumes, but we weren't allowed to put them on until we were getting ready to perform.

We rehearsed our Spanish Christian songs and took it very seriously. For a short while, we were in the public eye and were on television with the most famous children's show actor named, Cepillin (**Ricardo González Gutiérrez** known as **Cepillín** (born in Monterrey, Nuevo León) is a Mexican clown (*payaso*) as well as a singer, TV host and actor. Ricardo was a dentist who started to paint his face so that kids would not be afraid of him as he worked on their teeth. He became famous when a local TV channel interviewed him. The name *Cepillín* means little (tooth) brush, "cepillo" ("de dientes") in Spanish. With Televisa he had a show called *El Show de Cepillín*. This show was an educational, comedy and interview shows with guests such as Lou Ferrigno (who was *Hulk* on the popular TV show). The show was a success in Mexico as well as Chile and Puerto Rico. He arguably became the most famous clown in Mexico. Cepillín also recorded children songs (all information referenced from Wikipedia, the free encyclopedia). We did a commercial for toothpaste with Cepillin. They gave us all new toothbrushes and toothpaste and asked us to first brush our teeth before we made the commercial.

Lindsey and Dad played the guitar together often. He was left-handed but played right-handed. I am also left-handed and Lindsey was really patient with me and taught me to play right-handed. Even though I passed my free "sister sessions," I appreciated her but still didn't really enjoy playing the guitar. Lindsey had a beautiful voice and I think that made playing the guitar even more fun for her. Lindsey would impress our visitors, and since I didn't sing very well I usually ended up showing off how many jalapeños I could eat out of the jar. Nobody knew that since I sucked my thumb until I was eight, Mom had to dip my thumb in jalapeño juice all the time as a deterrent. My secret was that I liked it!

Emily was smart even as a toddler. Her solos were a special treat for our audiences. She sang a beautiful song called "Mira Me." She was three years old and she sang with a soft, confident, and adorable voice. The song seemed like it was written for a small child to sing. Lindsey worked hard at developing her beautiful voice and sang with pride. She also sang solos of her favorite songs and the audience loved her!

Spankings and humiliating punishment were techniques that the cult believe in and abused. Lindsey, Emily, Andretti, Luigio and I all got spankings—you could call some of them beatings depending on the spanking. Sometimes dad lined us up and spanked us one by one, it's a bad memory visualizing my brothers and sisters with their hands on the wall scared to death screaming while getting the spankings, it was one of the things that broke my heart to watch (I guess we were all in trouble for the same thing or at the same time, who knows).

Lindsey, Emily, and I would get so upset when he would whip our little brothers with his belt. We didn't think they needed spankings, and they were so little. I remember going up to Dad crying and pulling on his shirt, just like it was yesterday saying,

"Dad, please don't . . . just spank me instead, it will mean the same thing, I promise"

After our spanking, Dad would always take time to talk to each of us and tell us how much he loved us and why he had to spank us. He would say-

"Honey, now you know it hurts me more than it hurts you to give you this spanking. God says, "Spare the rod spoil the child."

Afterwards, we hugged and kissed and knew he loved us even though he had hurt us.

It turned out that these spankings were more cult ritual than disciplinary tactic.

We talked about God a lot and we believed in him. We prayed on our hands and knees when we really needed his help with something, like when I lost my glasses. Dad led our family meetings when he was around. He would always point out who had recently disobeyed him and how severe their punishment was going to be. Then he would be positive and talk about which one of his kids had done something sacrificial that week like volunteering to go with him to litness and help ask for family provisions. We were just six young kids back then, but he had our attention and expected us to take him seriously. At the end of the meeting, he would read the Bible to us and he would encourage us to love the Lord and memorize our Bible verses. He would also ask if any of us had a testimony that they wanted to share with the family.

Lindsey and I received immunization shots when we were babies that made us sick with extremely high fevers and caused us to have bad eyesight. We started wearing glasses at age four, but we lost our glasses a lot and it caused our vision to worsen over time. I spent most of my childhood squinting in order to see. It seemed like I was always losing my glasses and when Dad saw me without them, he would say-

"Abigail, where are your glasses?"

He always got mad at me when I wasn't wearing them. I said I didn't know, and he looked at me and put his hands on his belt buckle (a lot of times Dad just had to act like he was going to take off his belt and spank us). One time I said-

"*Wait*! "I think I know where they are; let me go get them."

I ran back to my bedroom and got on my hands and knees next to my dresser and prayed. I said-

"Thank you, Jesus; I love you, Jesus. Can you please, please, please help me find my glasses?"

I was in a big hurry and didn't have time for a long prayer. I opened my eyes and saw my glasses right there under the dresser and was so happy and said-

"Thank you very much, Jesus."

When our birthdays came around, we never expected anything because we knew we just didn't have any extra money. It didn't seem to bother us; it was the way we lived. Mom was always doing little things that made us happy, though. She would ask us about the things we wanted to have and the things we wanted to do, and she tried to work things out so that some of our wishes would come true. For example, she would say,

"Well, honey, we can make that on my sewing machine," or "Why don't we bake something really special together?"

We were always going places that were really fun (and free). The village festivals and carnivals were a lot of fun at night. There were colorful lights and huge piñatas everywhere. The crowded parades were so entertaining for all of us.

> *"The best inheritance a parent can give his children is a few minutes of his time each day."—O.A. Battista*[19]

I remember there was a fancy water park that was made of natural stone. It was in a nice neighborhood close to where we lived, and we used to sneak in through the bushes and ride the waterslides. That was one of the most thrilling things I remember doing in the summer. We had a plan to keep getting back on the waterslide until someone figured out that we hadn't paid and kicked us out. Every time we went around one waterslide lap, I

---

[19] Orlando Aloysius Battista (June 20, 1917-October 3, 1995), was a Canadian-American chemist and author who began writing at the age of twelve.

would look around and was surprised that nobody was asking us to leave. So when we went there, we did feel guilty but we got to stay all day long. Somehow Mom located a picture of Lindsey climbing one of the rock waterfalls at this very same water park, I love looking at that picture.

Mom had her special way to help us understand why it was important to work together and help out so we could free up our time to have fun.

We loved it when she read us the Little Red Hen story and asked her to read it to us over and over again. She used it in her family motivational speeches to inspire us to help her. It's a story about a little Red Hen that laid an egg and wanted to use it to bake a loaf of bread. The little Red Hen went outside and told her farm animal friends, "I'm going to make bread. Who wants to help me pick a kernel of wheat?" All the farm animals said, "Not me." She asked,

"Who wants to help me grind the wheat?" All the farm animals said,

"Not me."

She asked, "Who wants to help me make dough?" All the farm animals said, "Not me." She asked, "Who wants to help me bake it? All the farm animals said, "Not me." She said, "Then I'll do it myself." The bread was done baking and the whole farm smelled like delicious bread. She took it out of the oven and went outside and asked, "Who wants to help me eat it?" And all the farm animals said "Me!"

She said, "No!

You didn't want to help me pick the kernel of wheat, grind the wheat, make the dough, or bake it so I'll eat it myself." I still think about this story to this day, especially when I'm busy and someone asks for my help.

Mom was pregnant with Stefano. By this time the Mexican government was arresting and deporting a lot of foreign, controversial cult members. Dad put Mom, all six of us kids and another young couple on a train and sent us to our sweet Gram. I guess we stayed a little too long at Gram's home and she knew that if we were ever going to be out on our own again we would at least need something to live in and a car. She was an independent responsible single older woman, she was also frugal. It must have been hard for sweet Gram to make up her mind about how to help us but she ended up buying us a pop-up trailer and financed a Chevy Suburban to pull the trailer. The best part about the pop-up trailer was that we found that when it was totally folded down it had just enough space in the middle of the trailer top to safely place mom's rocking chair that Gram gave her when she had baby Lindsey. Since we were able to take it with us when we left Gram's, Mom always used it to nurse and rock the babies. She loved having it everywhere we went, especially at the camp grounds. She rocked Lindsey and I in it too, I guess she didn't want us to feel like we were too big to be in her special mommy chair.

1978 Cuernavaca, Mexico

We moved to Cuernavaca Mexico, where **Stefano** was born in August 1978. When Stefano (baby number seven) was born Lindsey was 11 years old, I was 10, Emily was 7, Andretti was 6, Luigio was 4 and Sebastian Jr. was almost 2 (give or take a few months for each age).

Cuernavaca[20] was a beautiful place to live. It is a town in Morelos (Mexico) also known City of Eternal Spring. In our neighborhood, there were flowering trees on every street and breathtaking hills everywhere. We were living in a house that had a beautiful backyard with a terrace that overlooked open acreage where a raven lived. We went on adventures

---

[20] "A famous vacation place among tourists due to its comfortable year-round climate, beautiful parks and gardens, as well as its convenient location within the country. This state capital comes to life on weekends, where local life is combined with the presence of the floating population that comes, mostly, from Mexico City. The heart of the city is the central plaza and palace. Each night of the week you can enjoy dancers, musicians, acrobats . . .", from Wikitravel. More about Cuernavaca; "It was established at the archeological site of Guadupita I by the Olmec, "the mother culture" of Mesoarmerica, approximately 3200 years ago." The Olmec were the first major civilization in Mexico, from Wikipedia.

walking down to the open acreage and had scavenger hunts. We found a lot of neat things we had never seen before like special types of clothes and shoes. We also found beautiful pottery left behind that had belonged to people that lived in the area.

When we had our family outings we went to the Cuernavaca religious celebrations; that was such an exciting time for us all! These celebrations were festivals that had fairs, fireworks shows, floats and dance performances.

Some of the amazing Cuernavaca festivities we got to enjoy were; El Dia de San Antonio, La Fiesta de Nuestra Senora de Los Milagros, Virgin of Guadalupe Day and Carnival. Carnival is a Tradition since 1965 and is celebrated in the days before Ash Wednesday. All the festivities had hundreds of people that attended to celebrate the traditions.

We also enjoyed going to the Cuernavaca Mercado. El Mercado[21] is a forty-five year old Mercado that was said to be the most important shopping mercados in the state of Morelos.

Dad started pulling away from us more than ever. At that time he had three girlfriends. Mom pretty much gave up on him; she was tired and worn out with the relationship and with life in general. We still loved and missed Dad and tried hard to make him feel happy when he was around. We somehow felt his distance was partly our fault.

Things were different for us now. Dad was earning money from somewhere and we were able to hire a nice Mexican lady that came to help us. This lady washed Stefano and Sebastian's cloth diapers outside on the washboard. I helped her out sometimes because it was fun using the washboard, but I

---

[21] "The Cuernavaca Mercado (market) is a sprawling thing that winds around and up and down. Very easy to get lost in. It's location in an arroyo (creek) just about 6 blocks east of downtown and the plaza. Much of it seems underground with many alleys that bring you up to city streets. Just about everything is for sale but mostly divided into sections of flower sellers, meat, vegetable, herbs, clothes and music. By SPARKS_MEX, LinkWithin.

was glad that it was not my job to wash all those smelly, dirty diapers. It seemed like we didn't have as many chores to do as we used to.

The parents of our friends next door were never home. They had a nice home and we went over there all the time. We played whatever creative games we thought of to entertain ourselves. Lindsey was the boss of our games; she had a great imagination and told all the kids how to play. Our friends showed us how to play spin the bottle—we had never played that game before. It was really fun for us to do all the things you had to do when you play spin the bottle. Some of those things we didn't let Emily do because she was three years younger than us.

Our family performed for the governor of Cuernavaca and we started to spend time with his family. They invited us to their home and we would play and swim with their children. When we performed for them, the governor's wife loved it and would say,

"Qué divino, qué divino."

Photo of Elizabeth, Lindsey, Sophia, Emily, Andretti, Luigio and baby Sebastian Jr. after a musical performance

They introduced us to their friend who operated a private school. Although we had a little room set up as a school room in our home, it was supposed to be Dad's job to "home school" us, and Mom's job to take care of the younger kids and babies. Dad was always too busy and never had the time to teach us. So we started attending the private school. I'm not sure, but I guess since we were trying to pull away from the COG, Mom had more control over the things we did, and that's why we went to this school. Still, it was difficult for my parents to make decisions independent of the COG's agenda.

We had to wear the school uniforms and for two weeks we were absolutely miserable! It did not make any sense to Lindsey and I why school was so hard. We thought that because we knew Spanish fluently and all our friends spoke only Spanish that school would be fun. All my classes except one were in Spanish, but we could not read or write in Spanish. I had one English class, and this class was just as bad as the Spanish classes since I couldn't read or write in English either. We thought we were somewhat educated, but we realized then that we didn't know nearly enough.

All my teachers announced that they were fortunate to have an American student in their class and that they wanted everyone to be friendly toward me. In my English class, the teacher told all the kids not to feel bad if I knew all the answers because I was an American. She would ask me questions, and I didn't know what she was talking about. She was confused and I was confused, then she asked me to read what was on the board in English to the class, and I tried to figure out how to read it, but got it wrong. This was the beginning of many years of experiencing shame and humiliation due to my lack of education at the time.

We were in school for the first time in Mexico; I can still remember that exact horrible humiliated anxiety I felt. While I was sitting in my classes I hoped to find Lindsey on my way to my next class, but I never did. We had outside courtyard recess right after my English class and I knew I could find her then.

Immediately when we finished my English class, I dashed out the door and ran to the courtyard desperately looking for Lindsey, *my best friend and the only person on the earth that knew how I felt!*

The first couple days when I found her in the courtyard I ran to her and cried on her shoulder. She also cried and we were both talking over each other about our embarrassing experiences. When our recess time was up, we hugged and had to say goodbye.

I was also mad that we couldn't be in the same classes together; we were always together and she was like my guardian angel. They said that she had to be in a different grade and we had different classes, at the time I didn't understand what that really meant. I thought it was a bunch of stupid rules.

Every day we had school it was the same routine. Even though all the kids were dressed the same, she was really easy to find because she stood out. She was the only tall girl with blonde hair in the crowds.

We were forced to stay in school for two weeks even though we were miserable. When Mom picked us up, our faces were red with humiliation and tears. I started a little game to help me get by until the two weeks were up. When teachers asked me questions, I would respond with a question, and that would distract everyone.

Later, when I started school for real in fifth grade, I played that same game and learned lots of other tricks, but I still felt like it was obvious to people that I was illiterate. All the kids and teachers had trouble understanding why on earth we didn't know anything and couldn't read or write.

After this horrible experience, many things really started to worry Mom. She couldn't stand or accept the fact that we were not educated and that we had been so sheltered that exposure to society hurt us so deeply. To me this school experience showed me how different our lives really were compared to other children.

She had been trying for a long time to pull us away from the cult. We managed to make several fresh starts alone, but the cult's power over Mom and Dad was too strong. Mom knew our lifestyle was not healthy for us and she wanted to escape the COG once and for all and start our new life in the United States.

CHAPTER 8

Mom and Us Seven Kids Left Behind in Mexico

My parents had already been having problems with raising our family under the cult's rules, but this was the moment that drastically changed the course of our lives. Mom had convinced my dad to move us back to the United States.

He decided to leave by himself to Texas and left all of us behind (Mom, Lindsey, Emily, Andretti, Luigio, Sebastian Jr., Stefano and me).

The idea was that Dad had to first go back and find a job so that we could have money to rent a house. My dad left and moved to Texas while we stayed in Mexico. One of Dad's girlfriends moved to Texas with him, but we had no idea that she was still with him.

Before Dad left, he told us that it was God's will to have a member named Francisco come live with us while he was in the United States and that God showed him in prophesy that Francisco's responsibility was to watch over us, protect us, and help provide for us according to his faith. Dad also promised to send Mom money to pay the rent.

Francisco moved in with us in Mexico and helped our family. Soon Mom looked up to him and appreciated him for being there. We were all still waiting to hear back from Dad because we wanted to start our new life in Texas and reunite with him. He had been gone for months and we had not heard from him. Francisco did what he could to raise money to get food, but there was never enough to pay for rent or buy what we needed. During the day, Mom would fix us rice and tortillas with frijoles and eggs, but at night we often went to bed hungry. The rent was months past due and we were being evicted.

It was Christmas time and our neighbors were talking about the gifts they were getting for Christmas and how excited they were. On Christmas Eve we had still not heard from Dad and were so disappointed; it was a very tough time for us. We knew we did not have a penny to our name and didn't even talk about Christmas. That night, Mom fed us beans and rice and we went to sleep. Mom had secretly tucked away instant milk, instant cheesecake, and cake and eggnog mixes. While we were sleeping she went through all her stuff and pulled out all the instant boxes and packs she could find. Lindsey woke up at 4:00 a.m. from the smell of baked food. She went in the kitchen and could not believe her eyes; Mom had been up all night making a surprise Christmas for us.

She baked a fancy cheesecake, strawberry cake, and a pie out of lemons, sugar, and cornstarch (she had cut the lemons from our neighbor's yard). She mixed powdered milk and eggs to make eggnog. Mom had cut down a poinsettia tree (three feet tall) and decorated it with hand-cut snowflakes she made from newspaper. She wrote a love note to each of us and tied it to the tree with small pieces of embroidery thread. She blew up a few balloons and placed them on top of the table. Lindsey looked around and thought it was so beautiful.

Under our poinsettia Christmas tree, she placed socks dolls that she made from our socks for the girls. They were inside sock doll beds she had made from oatmeal canisters she had used for storing things. She made the boys puppets and had put them under the tree also. Lindsey was overjoyed to say the least and couldn't wait to see the look on our faces when we saw it. When everyone was up, we sang songs together, ate all the sweets, and drank the eggnog. We played with our toys and were so thankful to Mom.

That Christmas turned out to be one of the most memorable ones for us! Later that evening we were also surprised by our neighbors; they came over and brought us gifts and a Christmas dinner.

"Keep your face in the sunshine and you cannot see the shadows."—
Helen Keller[22]

Mom finally got hold of Dad and begged him to send us the money we needed. She also told him she was planning to go back to Texas with the children and she expected him to find a house and have it fully furnished, with a pantry full of food for us when we arrived. She was enraged at him for not keeping in touch or sending us money to live on, and Dad promised her that he would do exactly what she asked.

Days went by and there was no word from Dad. Mom made up her mind to pick up and move back to the United States once and for all!

She knew what she had to do if she was ever going to escape the cult life. She had faith that she could make this big break alone with her seven children, but she knew the journey would be rough.

We packed our Suburban with the most important things we owned and everything else we could, which wasn't too much since all eight of us also had to squeeze in the car. We left everything else behind.

Dad didn't know we were on our way back to Texas.

Our family—Mom, Lindsey Star, Emily Knight, Andretti, Luigio, Sebastian Jr., Stefano, and I—were on our way to a new life. Mom had plans for us and made the first step in our journey to victory!

"The positive thinker sees the invisible, feels the intangible,
and achieves the impossible."—**Winston Churchill**

---

[22]   Helen Keller (1880—1968), she began a writing career while a student at Radcliffe. In 1903, she wrote The Story of My Life.

CHAPTER 9

Returning to the US and Enduring Severe Upheaval

1978 United States

Texas

We drove from gas station to gas station. We witnessed, sang songs, and asked for donations of food and gas to get us back to the United States.

While traveling from Cuernavaca to Mexico City all our family pictures, personal items and keepsakes, like our beautiful handmade Mexican puppets, were stolen out of our car. All of our pictures from the toothpaste commercial with Cepillin and other performances were gone.

We were robbed of the photos and personal items, memories of our proudest moments and all the wonderful things we did and amazing people we met. The special clothes Mom had made for us were also gone.

As with other moments of devastation, we all prayed and talked about what had happened. Sometimes when we did this, it was a big relief. We would ask Jesus to wipe away our tears. We said whatever was in our hearts and when we were done, we opened our eyes and felt like someone had sprinkled magic dust over us and we felt at peace.

When we were crossing the border to the United States, Sebastian was sucking his thumb and twirling his hair around his finger. The border patrol woman said in English-

"Hey, little boy what's your name?"

Sebastian wouldn't take his thumb out of his mouth. She said-

"Can I have some of that?"

He shook his head no and kept sucking his thumb. She said-

"If you keep sucking that thing you're gonna swallow it."

Sebastian took his thumb out of his mouth and said-

"I know."

Mom got in contact with Dad . . . . he wasn't prepared for our arrival.

Mom was going to hold Dad to his word and wanted to know where the new house was. She wanted to make sure it had furniture and food in it. Dad told Mom that he really didn't have a house yet, so we ended up at the Red Roof Inn for a couple weeks. The hotel room only had one bed, and Dad had his girlfriend with him and she also had a young son. It was horrible for us because we missed Dad, but were emotionally overwhelmed with disappointment because we thought we were going to be a family again. Instead, he had a new woman with him and we had to live with her and Mom together.

Mom was ready more than ever to take control of her life and the destiny of her children. She was prepared and decided to follow through with her plan to educate us and acclimate us into society. But first she had to deal with Dad. He was still into the cult and he wanted to hold onto what he had been brainwashed to believe and the seniority he had worked hard to get. He wanted to go back to the cult and take mom and a second wife (what he should have done is left the cult right at that point and help us rebuild our life). Staying in this motel was the hardest on mom. She slept on the floor with us and Dad and his girlfriend got the bed.

Dad found a house for us to rent. We all moved in and it was the same set-up for a while—Dad and his girlfriend had their own bedroom. Mom slept on the floor in the girls' room. Every one of us were struggling to keep our sanity. Mom hadn't decided how to deal with Dad. She wanted to convince him to leave his girlfriend, but if that didn't work she was getting ready to kick them out. But first she needed to figure out how to earn the money to support us.

Lindsey, Emily, Andretti, Luigio, and I had to start public school and we were a little excited but really freaked out about it. My baby brothers Sebastian, who was two, and Stefano, who was under one year old, didn't know what the hell was going on so they were probably not too bad off. Dad started a new business called Completion Enterprise. It was a service-oriented business that cleaned homes to make ready for sale. He hired a crew of illegal immigrants to work for him.

Mom tried to keep us organized like when we lived in Mexico. We used to have family meetings where we would gather together in the living room. We would take turns talking about the chores we did and things that bothered us. In Mexico, my dad led the meetings and he was very structured about the things he needed to talk about. I think he took it too seriously. It made us very mature because he told us about what was going on and the problems the family was having.

Dad had not yet moved out of the house and things were in total chaos. We were in a strange transition between the missionary cult life and the sinner society life. But we knew that we wanted to take the good and leave the bad, so our plan was to start public school, start to reverse some of the brainwashing that the cult taught us, pray, and keep Jesus in our hearts. And somehow we needed to figure out the big things, like how to make enough money to have a place to live, groceries, money to take care of our old car, and gas. Mom got a good job working as a waitress and immediately went to the Goodwill and bought us bunk beds. We really wanted a little black and white television, so Mom got us one. Right away, we all got real sick from the food in Texas; we all had heartburn. We were used to eating tortillas, rice and beans. We also ate a lot of spicy candy and chicharrones[23] in Mexico.

Lindsey and I were placed in different schools because she was in sixth grade and I was in fifth grade, but we both hated school. Mom talked to Lindsey and me before our first day and told us what to say. She tried to prepare us for our experience. She wrote my first and last name down on a piece of paper so I could know what to tell the teacher. In Mexico we didn't use our last name, and since my Bible name was Abigail, I didn't go by Sophia.

On my first day of school, we were lined up outside the playground and the teacher was taking our names one by one. I was so nervous about my turn because I had lost the piece of paper that Mom had given me with the spelling of my first and last name. I honestly couldn't even remember what my last name was.

My turn came up and the teacher asked me my name and I said Sophia. I said I couldn't remember my last name but my first name was definitely Sophia. She asked me how to spell it and I said, "Um, well, uh," and then the kids behind me started guessing for me how to spell Sophia, and I kept saying, "Oh yeah, that's right." Then someone would spell it differently, and I would say, "Oh, yeah, that's it." I wished that I could just tell her my name was Abigail because I knew how to spell that.

The kids were so mean and called us all kinds of names that we did not understand. They called Lindsey "cow lips," which made me want to laugh but she was sad when she told me, so I didn't. When Lindsey and I wore our glasses, kids called us "four eyes". I didn't understand why wearing glasses meant that we had four eyes. We wore our long Mexican dresses with leather sandals and didn't know a thing about what kids were like in

---

23   Chicharrón is a snack food made from pork skin deep fried with seasonings, very popular in Mexico

the U.S. Back in Mexico everyone loved us and wanted to be our friends even though it must have been hard for them to accept the crazy things that came out of our mouths about our lifestyle. We didn't have to worry about being around kids that would make fun of us and humiliate us in public.

The kids at school noticed that our mannerisms weren't anything they had ever seen before and they labeled us outcasts and weirdoes. We were struggling all over the place as we learned more and more about the real world. One day a boy and girl from my class chased me while walking home, threw me down on the ground, and the girl held my arms back and told the boy to hit me. I said, "I rebuke you and if you harm me you will have to answer to God." I wiggled out of her hands and got away and ran about a hundred miles an hour all the way home.

This was my first realization of how mean kids could be in the United States. Once the kids in our neighborhood got to know us, they invited us to their house to jump on their trampoline. We knew that our family was a lot of fun to play with and that's why they liked us. They invited us to eat with them and play in their homes. We became friends with the kids on our block and it was so nice.

We had a cousin that lived not too far from us named Lynn, and we were so excited that we had an American family member that was our age. We thought she would like us because she was our cousin. Even though we had not met her yet, it was a relief to us. We used to play with her when Lindsey and I were babies, but I did not remember her. Lynn came to our home to visit and she was so beautiful and sweet. She loved us instantly and we were so comforted by her presence.

The next time she came over, she brought her seashell collection. She showed it to me and the shells were shiny pastel colors. When I looked at them I couldn't believe how beautiful they were and felt special that she was sharing them with me. I knew I didn't have anything special to show her, but still I asked her,

"Do you want to see my shell collection?"

She said yes. So I told her I would be right back. I snuck outside the front door and went to the ditch and scraped up some muddy broken shells. I ran back and washed them in the kitchen and put them in a bowl. I showed them to her and I must have had a look of pride on my face because she looked surprised and curious. I asked her,

"Do you like my shell collection?"

"Yes, I really do."

She didn't know us at all but she was very sweet.

Lindsey learned a bunch of new curse words right away and was going around the house teaching them to us. She would make sentences out of them and I could not figure out where on earth she learned them. After months of cursing lessons, Lindsey would tease me because she knew that I still didn't get some of the phrases. For example she would tell me that it was my job to clean our bedroom the whole week, and I would get pissed off and tell her,

"Like hell I won't."

She always caught on so quickly to everything. I always looked up to her and still do. We started to get addicted to watching every single thing that came on TV—*Gilligan's Island, I Dream of Jeanie, Charlie's Angels,* and all the other shows from the late 70s. I fell in love with Eric Estrada.

Present day when I talked about these memories of our life with my cousin Lynn she said;

> "I remember seeing my Aunt sleeping on the floor in the dining room."

> "I remember when I was visiting one time we had less than 1 lb of ground beef and we were all hungry. Lindsey got an egg and made the meat spreadable. She spread her mixture

like butter on hamburger buns and placed the meat side down in a frying pan and cooked them. THEY WERE DELICIOUS. I couldn't believe how creative she was with food! Also, we all wanted a snack but we only had a little tiny bit of chocolate cake. She gave us each a large spoon full of cake and poured milk over it. I eat cake like this to this day! It is so good!"

"I remember that place like it was yesterday. Due to the fact that I was so young and didn't know you guys very well, I didn't understand why my uncle was in that room, in the dark with someone other than my aunt"

"I remember being very scared at night. One big thing was . . . . trying to go to the bathroom with all of us! There was one bathroom, 5 young ones, 3 teenagers and 3 adults; it was hard. I was an only child and never had that problem!"

Mom finally kicked Dad and his girlfriend out of our house! The whole ordeal was so traumatic for us. She had had enough and wasn't going to put up with Dad's crap any longer. We were going to school. So many things were happening to us (all at once).

We didn't have enough money to pay our rent, so we got evicted and moved into an apartment. After that we lived in lots of different apartments. Mom had to tell the apartment managers that she only had four kids. She made it a rule that we could not play outside all at the same time, but this was too hard for us to do, and we kept getting asked to move. Dad disappeared and we did not hear from him for a long time.

1980 Texas

Mom decided to send for Francisco, who was living back in Cuernavaca. Francisco moved into an apartment and started working as a waiter in an

Italian restaurant. Later he came to live with us and married Mom. We started to call him Papa.

Lindsey and I were bored teenagers, thirteen and fourteen. One day, we were walking to the Stop-N-Go, but we never made it there. We had a long way to walk and we were getting sweaty and tired. A white truck drove by with a pile of young people in the back. As they drove by, they were screaming and whistling at us. It caught us off guard and we got scared. Lindsey always had an instant reaction to things, and she knew how she wanted to handle the situation.

She was mad and immediately gave them "The Bird". I said-

"Lindsey, why did you do that?"

The truck loudly slammed on its breaks. It turned around and headed for us. I said-

"Oh no, they're coming to get us. You pissed them off; you should have never shot them the finger." Lindsey said-

"So what, I don't care. Let them come get us."

Lindsey was always courageous. Still, we both started to tremble as they drove closer to us. Lindsey said-

"Okay, I'm going to pretend I'm from Russia and start talking a foreign language, and you tell them I thought that was the way to say hello!"

The truck stopped right in front of us and kicked up a cloud of dirt. Everyone got out of the truck and gathered all around us. We thought they were going to beat us up bad. The guy driving the truck looked at Lindsey and said-

"Why did you flip us the finger?"

Lindsey looked at me and said something that sounded like a cross between Chinese and Spanish. I translated to the guy and tried to get them to believe that Lindsey didn't speak English and that she really thought that giving people the bird was a way of saying hello. I told them that she didn't know how we do things in the United States. They told me that I'd better teach her about what the finger means because we could get hurt really bad from doing that. I said-

"Oh, I know" and "Yes, I will."

And they got in the truck and drove off. We were worried that they were going to change their minds and turn back around. We walked really fast at first and then ran all the way home.

Mom was waitressing double shifts at a restaurant and Francisco was working as a waiter and going to technical school, pursuing a degree in electronics. It was very difficult for us financially with no help from Dad and little money coming in. Lindsey and I went to Holly Woods Junior High, Holly Branch Junior High, and Campwood Junior High. We moved into about five different apartments in one year. In junior high, Lindsey and I were separated and that is when we began to take different paths in life.

We handled our rejection and took our abuse from others differently. I would fail almost all my classes every year. Mom would make sure that the principals would pass me; she explained to them that I had been a victim of circumstance and lacked an education because I had spent my last seven years as a missionary's daughter in Mexico. She begged them to work with us and help us make it through school. Mom insisted that they pass us and promised we would eventually catch up.

It was a horrible thing for me to be called on in class by my teachers. I had personality, but people got the wrong impression of me. I lived in fear almost the entire time I was in school. I had so much anxiety about being singled out and asked a question. When I tried to answer a question and was corrected by someone, I would laugh and say, "Of course, I knew that, that was so easy . . ." I was always trying to cover up what I did not understand and I got used to things being that way.

To make matters worse, I didn't wear my glasses to school because I did not want the extra criticism, so I could not see the chalk board. Even if I sat in the first desk of the classroom, I was still blind as a bat. My glasses were right in my purse, but I didn't dare put them on. I often wished that I could put them on for a second, just to see the chalkboard. If I had, I might have been able to a figure out what was going on.

Mom and stepdad Francisco fought all the time. Mom became pregnant with baby number eight. Mom was still under the influence of the COG beliefs about birth control. Women were taught that any type of birth control was considered murder.

One evening the boys were asleep in there room. The girls were sleeping in their room and our cousin Lynn was visiting us. We heard a lot of yelling and screaming. Mom ran in our room and locked the door. Francisco banged on the door and yelled at mom to come out. He was very drunk. She was very pregnant and had hit her badly. We opened the window and climbed down. We all were getting out the window and he had gone outside and came around the corner. Some guys were outside and it scared him off. We got Mom out the window and ran to a neighbor's.

In 1980, Mom and Francisco had their first child together. They named our new baby sister **Madeleine.** We had not had any new additions to the family for years and were not use to having a tiny baby in the family.

We were struggling all over the place. We didn't have much furniture, and there was hardly enough money for rent and groceries. When my friends came over, they asked me what happened to all our furniture and I said-

"Um, well . . . oh, my mom just took all our furniture to get cleaned."

Then they would open the refrigerator door to grab a snack and asked where all our food was. I said-

"Oh yeah, I know. Mom was just about to go to the grocery store."

For a couple months, this popular, pretty girl made fun of me every day on the school bus. I never knew what to say, so I just cried. One day, she was at it again. She was making fun of my clothes, hair, makeup, and shoes. She was really hurting my feelings and suddenly I turned and started to scream at her. I said,

"Just go ahead and say all those means things to make me cry because you don't care if my feelings hurt. You don't care if I hurt so bad that I can't stand myself and want to die. You say all those mean things to me and I've never once said anything to hurt your feelings because I don't want to hurt your feelings."

She looked at me for a few seconds as if she had seen a ghost. Everything was very quiet and everyone was waiting to hear what she was going to say to me. She started to utter a word and said,

"I'm sorry."

It was strange to me because every day after that she asked me to sit with her when I got on the bus.

Soon Andretti and I were having another birthday. Mom told me that for my birthday she was going to give me a disco party because I just loved disco. I thought it was a nice thing for her to say, but I knew that she couldn't afford it and that probably nobody would come to my party anyway. Still, she planned the party. When I came home from school one day she had the living room decorated with a strobe light in the middle of the room and a beautiful birthday cake for Andretti and I. She had taken a Wilton cake decorating class so she could decorate cakes and sell them, but this time the cake was for *me* and my brother! I didn't know what to say or what to do. I was so excited.

Mom had already invited some of the neighborhood kids. After I looked around the party scene I quickly dashed outside and told *all the kids* on the street that I was having a party and that everyone should come!

All the kids came running over and we started the music and the party began, it was so much fun. The party lasted for hours; nobody in our neighborhood had ever been to a party like this one (it was the best time for my brothers and sisters). All the kids were talking about it for weeks and kept asking me when my mom was going to give me another party.

Later on there were several other kids in our family that were given special birthday cakes. One year for Luigio's birthday mom baked him a cool guitar cake. We still have the picture of it and he is holding his "guitar birthday cake" with a huge smile on his face. She also baked our cousin Lynn a *Ziggy* cake for her birthday and it was a big surprise to her. Ziggy was her favorite cartoon character. We were so excited about it and when we gave it to her she was so happy and couldn't believe that we had made this fancy Ziggy cake just for her. Lynn's parents were not getting along and she was very sad during this time in her life. She said;

"You guys are my second family and like my brothers and sisters"

Through all the turmoil, Mom stayed positive and also taught us to be that way. She talked to us about our problems and made us feel good about the things we were struggling with. She comforted us by explaining that everything happening in our lives, including hers, was just temporary. She said that we would grow up and have wonderful husbands and live in nice big houses. She had a special way of reaching deep into our little, broken hearts and healing us.

CHAPTER 10

Fighting to Adapt, Survive and Integrate into Society

Francisco (Papa) was still a waiter and going to school. They had a really bad marriage and he just couldn't handle the responsibility of such a large family, and he didn't want to. He was drinking and smoking pot at night. He resented the fact that our dad just dumped the responsibilities on him to provide and care for his seven children, and now he had his own child with Mom.

We continued to struggle through the adjustment of getting up in the mornings and would run around trying to get ready for school before we missed the school bus. The older girls would get the kids ready while Mom was busy taking care of the baby, fixing Francisco's lunch, and getting ready to take him to work. The pressure of getting everything done first thing in the morning was unbelievably frantic, but that was just the way we started off our day.

All of the girls slept in the same room sideways on a full-sized bed, like sardines, but sometimes we were passed out on the floor depending on which one of our brothers and sisters were crying in the middle of the night. Each morning, Mom came to us and, with a very gentle voice, said,

"Honey, it's time to get up."

She waited two seconds then said,

"Wake up, hurry. We have to get the kids ready. Hurry or you'll all miss the bus!"

After that Lindsey, Mom, and I had about five and a half minutes to run around like chickens with our heads cut off trying to wake up the kids and find clothes for them to wear to school. It was hard to keep the kids in clean clothes because we did not have a washer and dryer. Mom washed the cloth diapers every day and dried them by hanging them in front of the kitchen stove with the oven turned on.

Waking up the four boys and finding clothes was the biggest problem in the mornings. Our brothers were so adorable that I think we spoiled them too much. They never wanted to get up when we woke them in the morning. We pushed them out the front door while they were still half asleep. One of us would wake them up and Emily's job was to run around the house picking up wadded clothes from the corners of the rooms and behind the doors on the floor. It didn't matter if they were clean or dirty—we just needed to find something that fit.

The bus driver would be waiting outside nearby our home honking; we would hear him yelling from outside. Our hearts were pounding and we started to freak out. One of us would get on the bus to stall the bus driver, and the rest of us would run out. My brothers usually had their pants on but not snapped, and their shoes and shirts were in their hands. Their hair usually looked so funny sticking straight up, except for Sebastian. He seemed to always take more care of his personal appearance than the others; he combed his hair daily.

Kids at school started to talk a lot about going to the local roller skating rink. I really wanted to go, so I talked my parents into taking me a couple times. I absolutely loved it!

I couldn't stop talking about it and wanted to go all the time but of course we couldn't afford it. To no surprise, Mom fixed that problem and arranged for me to work there in the food service area. I was allowed to skate there for free on my breaks and I was also making money.

For me, roller skating was so much fun and made me really happy. I got to live out my fantasy of being a disco queen when I was on roller skates. I skated when I was working at the roller rink and I got to skate when my parents would drop me off just to skate.

Back in Mexico I would skateboard with the kids who lived on the block, we all skated really fast down a steep, long hill. I would go full speed ahead. I didn't know how I was going to stop, and didn't care. Most of the time I just jumped right off the skateboard because I was going so fast and there was no other way to stop.

Before our dad completely disappeared, we stayed with him on some weekends, and he would drop me off at the roller rink from time to time. Roller skating became a big part of me really fast! I learned new tricks and got faster every time I went. Mom encouraged all of us and said we were good at the things we liked to do, she also said;

"but it was true, you were all over-achievers and dedicated yourselves whole heartedly to whatever you did . . ."

When my parents would drop me off to skate I would go alone. It seemed like the kids there had friends with them, as I was waiting to get inside I was nervous about being alone but excited to skate (my heart started pounding and my hands started to get clammy). I could hardly wait to get my skates on and hit the disco floor. I was very self-conscious about being the only one that didn't have a friend and I thought kids would see me alone and know I did not have any friends. So, when I was in line to get in, I would start to act happy and start waving at the kids inside the roller rink. Once I got in and put my skates on, I was swept away. The music they played was the best ever! They played Donna Summer, Le Chic, Ring My Bell, I Love the Night Life, Le Freak, Ladies Night, Celebrate, Michael Jackson, and many more songs and artists.

On the days that I worked at the roller rink I got to skate before and after work and even on my breaks! Sometimes I got away with wearing my roller skates in the kitchen so I could have more time to skate on my break. Even though I felt like a cool kid when I was roller skating, I'm sure I looked ridiculous in the kitchen all sweaty, cooking hamburgers, slipping, sliding and falling all over the place with my roller skates on. The floor was greasy and it was really hard to move around with skates on. I injured myself more on the greasy floor in the kitchen with my roller skates than I did on the roller rink floor. I remember falling and hitting my head on the edge of the kitchen counter, running into the refrigerator and busting my knee and sliding not being able to stop and banging into the metal stove and bruised my hip and elbow.

In Mexico my friends and I had talked about how exciting it would be to be old enough to disco but back then I was not sure if I would live that long because Jesus would be returning soon and take me to heaven before I got big. After we had been out of the cult for a while, I figured out that the cult was wrong and Jesus was not coming back right away, so I would probably keep growing up.

Roller-skating was like being in a disco club for me, and I thought about it all the time when I was not at the rink. I tried everything I saw other kids doing. I was able to spin in the middle of the floor under the strobe light; I was able to do the so-called splits on skates, to skate in swirls spinning around while going straight, and to speed skate. I was really good and kids would sometimes watch me, and I could tell they thought I was really good. Sometimes when I would slow down to rest while skating, I would start to wave again at my imaginary friends that were across the room.

When Madeleine was a two day old newborn baby, Francisco came home drunk and beat Mom up. None of us kids where home that weekend (we were with my Dad). I got home shortly after they had their horrible fight. I looked at my mom and my heart sunk. Her jaw was crooked, her lips were swollen, she had a bloody nose, and her eye was red and purple. I was totally freaked out and horrified! I asked her what happened and she put the baby down and asked me not to say anything to Francisco. He came out of the bathroom and I had an enraged horrified look on my face. I said,

"I know you did that to my mom."

Shortly after Madeline was born we had to move out of our apartment. Mom had a huge responsibility and had to figure out what to do and where to go.

1980 Victoria, Texas

Dad told Mom that he would take care of us. Then all six of my other brothers and sisters went to stay with Dad for a while. Mom and Francisco moved out of the apartment and lived in their car for a while with baby Madeline. Francisco had finished his certification as an electronic technician but couldn't find a job. Mom and Francisco finally moved into a rundown, one-bedroom apartment where Francisco started working as a maintenance man.

Dad bought a brand new trailer and we moved to the country with him, his wife, and his stepson. Lindsey and I went to Victoria Junior High. Dad and our stepmom planned to start a new family with all of us, but we were miserable and wanted to be with Mom. Dad had bought this new trailer and we had new furniture, and we liked that. At first we were excited to have new, nice things. Dad even bought me a brand-new pair of roller skates.

He explained to all of us that he went through a lot of trouble and spent a lot of money to make us happy and start a new life with us. We understood what he told us and it was nice for a change to have money, but none of it mattered that much. After a while we couldn't stand it because we missed Mom so much and wanted to move back with her. We started fighting with our stepmom during the day when Dad was working. When he got home, she would tell him what had happened and he began to beat us with his belt again.

"Children will not remember you for the material things you
provided but for the feeling that you cherished them."
—Richard L. Evans[24]

Lindsey, Emily, Andretti, Luigio, Sebastian Jr., Stefano, and I moved in with Francisco, Mom, and Madeline in their one-bedroom apartment. They seemed to be getting along well and we were all so thrilled to be back with Mom. We told her everything that had happened when we were living with Dad and his wife, and she felt really bad and guilty about letting us live with him.

Shortly before we moved out of Dad's trailer, something wonderful happened with my sister, Lindsey in school. It is hard for me to describe how I felt when I watched it happen to her—it was surreal. Lindsey didn't make friends easily, but she didn't seem to care. She did the things that she wanted to do and wasn't shy (she was a true rebel). In Victoria, Lindsey was in eighth grade. She was self-conscious, but she was also confident and she knew she could sing. As I've mentioned, she had been singing ever since she was a little girl.

One day a talent show was announced on the intercom at Victoria Junior High, and she heard all the kids talking about what they would do for the talent show. Every day she saw kids practicing their acts. She never considered that she might be qualified to do something like enter a talent show, but something told her that she should take the chance. She went to the choir director and told him that she wanted to do the show.

He told her,

"The show is in two days and you don't even know what you are going to sing."

She said,

---

[24]   Richard L. Evans (Nov. 26, 1946-Nov. 14, 2010), writer best known for his inspirational messages.

"Well I know, can you play "The Rose", recorded by Bette Midler in 1979?"

He had a smile on his face and couldn't resist her and said that he promised to learn it. They agreed to meet the next day and he told Lindsey,

"If you can sing this song by tomorrow, I'll let you enter the talent show."

She showed up, sang the song, and he let her in the show. When the day of the show came, she wore a long dress to school. I was standing in the bleachers with all the other kids inside the gym, and I could not believe that Lindsey was about to sing. It happened so fast that I never had a chance to talk to her about it. I thought she got scared and changed her mind, but Lindsey was the last act to come on. While I was waiting for her turn, I felt very edgy and my hands were sweaty. I didn't know what to think. I was very excited and proud that my best friend and sister was good enough to perform, but I was also very scared that we were going to get really embarrassed.

Her turn was up. I watched her as she walked on the stage and up close to the edge. The gym was full of students and there was total silence. All kinds of things were going through my mind. I was worried for her, yet I couldn't believe she had the guts to be there! She held the microphone in her hand close to her mouth. She was calm, and the music started to play.

With a brave, beautiful, loud voice she sang "The Rose" perfectly!

Lindsey said,

"When it was my turn, I imagined I was in a movie, and that this was my moment to shine in front of everyone. I sang with my whole heart and the audience stood when it was over and clapped loudly."

Later that day, the school announced over the PA that Lindsey Santino had won first place in the talent show.

Another great moment was when our brother Andretti (who also was always singing as a little boy and still does), won the talent show in his elementary school, singing "The Shoemaker's Elf." He was so proud of himself and we were all proud of him!

> *"Taking risks helps you grow and makes* you *better than you think you are."—Unknown, 2009*

Mom's uncle had a successful family business and owned a vacant rental house and told us we could live in it for a while for free in exchange for doing repairs and fixing it up. The only problem was that it was in one of the most violent neighborhoods in the city. We moved into his house, and I went to McDonnell Middle School, one of the worst schools in the city. My great-uncle also wanted us to help him out in his nearby office when we could, to make up for the free rent.

One time Dad came over to visit and mom was very mad at him. She was about to hand him a jar of homemade salsa she made but instead she threw it at his leather jacket. It broke when it hit his jacket and splattered everywhere. I thought it was funny and the whole scene looked kind of cool but it really wasn't funny. We were all speechless and not use to seeing mom throw things at Dad, it was totally unplanned. I can't believe she wanted to give him that delicious salsa in the first place.

Dad and his new wife were still involved secretly with the cult. One day, he told Mom that he wanted to pick up Andretti and spend some alone time with him, but he never brought him home. When Dad didn't come back with Andretti, Mom got very worried. She tried to contact Dad, but no answer. She then went out looking for them and found that they had moved out of their house. Mom cried every day for three months, she never gave up hope that she would soon find her son.

She met a private investigator who offered to help her find Andretti, but Dad had changed his name and covered his tracks so well that the investigator could not find them. We were all devastated; we loved Andretti and missed him badly. Finally Mom received a letter in the mail from Oklahoma.

The letter read;

"Elizabeth, I am Jennifer's mother, and I know you have been missing your son, Andretti. Sebastian and Jennifer dropped him off here at our farm in Oklahoma three months ago and never came back to get him. He wants to be with you and his brothers and sisters, and we want to do the right thing and send him back to you. Please tell us how we can get him to you" Mom called the number in the letter, and they put Andretti on the plane to Texas the very next day.

CHAPTER 11

Adjusting to Life in the Inner City

1981 Inner City, Texas

Dad left for good and we didn't know where he went. I guess he thought he was doing what Abraham did in the Bible story and was sacrificing us for the Lord (or at least that is what I thought).

We started school in the new house. Our neighborhood (in our uncle's rental house) was predominately Black and Hispanic, which made me feel a little more comfortable about the school. Although you wouldn't think we would fit in because we were mostly blonde and blue-eyed, we felt comfortable being around Latinos, and they really liked us. Mom warned us that it was a bad neighborhood, but we did not really know what she meant.

There was a huge park in our neighborhood and there were signs posted about a Halloween Fair. There was going to be a costume contest. When we drove by and found out about it, there was no question that Mom was going to make all of us costumes and enter us in the contest. We were all super excited. It didn't take long for us to decide what we wanted to dress up as, and it was our number one priority that week. Mom and the older girls helped make all the costumes.

In the past, when we were members of the cult, the children would dress up for Halloween as characters from the Bible (Mary, Joseph, David, etc.)

and knock on the front doors of homes. Instead of saying "Trick or Treat," we would say, "Jesus Loves You." When they asked if we wanted candy we would say "No, thank you," and hand them the tri-folded pamphlets.

We were living our different life now, and were full of free will. We were allowed to decide what we wanted to dress up as for Halloween and it could be whatever we wanted. Lindsey was a Playboy Bunny, I was a Gypsy, Emily was a Wizard, Andretti was Dracula, Luigio was a pirate, Sebastian was a puppy dog, Stefano was the Tin Man, and Madeline was herself (an adorable little baby doll).

When I started school, Mom really encouraged me to be in all the sports activities they offered. I was in basketball, track, and the swim team. I even joined the pep squad. I was the only white girl in most of my classes, and I made some nice friends. Some of the Hispanic kids liked me, but the others were jealous that I was fluent in Spanish but still a white girl.

Overall, things were going good for me at school. Most of the Black kids liked me. They kept coming up to me and saying-

"Okay, so I hear you're not Mexican. Is that true?"

And I said—"Well, yeah not really." Then they said-

"But you have to be because you talk just like the Chicanos."

They thought it was really cool but did not want to ruin their reputation by showing it too much. It made me feel really good that they liked me.

Going to this school was a little break for me. It was nice to be around all those Mexican kids—it felt a little like home. I didn't feel paranoid about being singled out. Kids called me white girl and things like that, but I was glad that that's all they noticed about me. I had one teacher that was the best teacher in the whole school. She was a very beautiful and sweet art teacher named Mrs. Barbara Reynolds. She got all her kids involved in the most fun art projects. We made leather belts and wallets; we did macramé, pottery, and so much more. I looked forward to her class and so did all the other students. When Mrs. Reynolds class started, we all felt like little honored guest at someone's magical fun house. I remember so vividly watching her walk around the classroom checking on each student. She would find kids that need help and, for example say;

"Maria, can you please come over here and help Michael with designing his leather wallet; since you already finished yours and did a wonderful job"

When we left her class each day we felt either confident or proud that we made something very special or we looked forward to continue working on our project the next day.

Present day: I think about these great memories of Mrs. Reynolds from time to time and last Christmas I decided to call the school to see if she was still there so I could visit her. The front office told me that she was the only teacher that had not yet retired (from the teacher that taught the year I attended) and I could go visit her. This was her last year before her retirement and I was overjoyed that I didn't miss my chance to thank her for being such a wonderful teacher. When I arrived at the school, it was like a time warp all the way back to eighth grade. They told me where her room was, and I put on my visitor sticker and walked down those old halls. The school looked just like it did thirty years ago. I walked into her room, when I looked at her she was beautiful and still had her caring sweet smile. She welcomed me with open arms and said- "When they told me Sophia Santino was coming to visit me I thought to myself, *is that the little quiet white girl that was in my class that year?*" We had a wonderful visit.

About this time, I started to embrace life and reached out beyond what I had ever done before. I got really involved in all those sports teams and even worked in the front office. Mom encouraged me the whole way and wanted me to take advantage of everything I could. The only sport I was asked to leave was basketball and thought it wasn't because I was only four feet nine inches tall, but it was because I was really bad at it and was hurting the team. To be honest, I had never participated in group sports before, so I wasn't good at the other sports either, but the teams were nice to me and let me play.

"Success comes in cans. Failure comes in can't."
—*WILFRED PETERSON*[25]

The worst teacher in the whole school was my history teacher, Mrs. Jackson. She was always ridiculing me and making fun of me in class. I remember hearing her mumble and I didn't really understand what she was saying or what she meant, but she was always talking about me during class. She hated me. She would say-

"White girl, you don't belong here."

One day I was on my way to Mrs. Jackson's History class and walked in her classroom two seconds after the tardy bell rang, along with several other kids. We were all walking toward our seats, and I heard the teacher yelling. Then I heard Mrs. Jackson say-

"Yeah, you, white girl."

I knew that she couldn't be talking to me because I hadn't done anything wrong, but I was the only white girl in her class. I sat down and she kept yelling. Mrs. Jackson said-

"Hey, don't be coming to my class acting all like you can't hear me."

I said—"What, you were talking to me?"

Mrs. Jackson said—"Yeah, you know I'm talking to you."

I started to say something and she said—"Shut up."

---

[25] Wilfred Arlan Peterson (1900-1995), American author especially admired for his inspirational essays

I said—"What? You can't talk to me like that," and Mrs. Jackson said-

"Shut up, shut up, shut up, or I will have you picking your teeth off the floor one-by-one. That's right, I'll kick your ass, White Girl."

All the kids were in as much shock as I was. Next she started a history film and left the classroom. I was so humiliated and mad and the kids wouldn't stop staring at me. I became angrier as the minutes rolled by, and I replayed in my mind what she said to me.

Right then, I picked up my books went to the door of the class and looked down the hall to make sure it was clear. I ran as fast as I could down the hall. My heart was pounding and I was shaking all over and my legs felt like they were going to collapse, but I kept running. Kids were not permitted to leave the school during school hours, but I was going to run all the way home to Mom. I was able to make it all the way to the exit door without being seen. I felt like I was running to escape prison. I ran home as fast as I could.

On the way, I was so scared that the principal, Mr. Vasquez, would start running after me. I heard a man yelling and looked to my side, and it was Mr. Vasquez in his car. He was yelling-

"Come back here, girl," but I ignored him because I knew that he wanted to take me back to school and beat me or have that witch beat me. I took the short cut and he lost me. I got home and banged on the door, screaming for Mom to open it.

Mom was frantic. I finally calmed down enough to tell her the whole story. Just then, we heard a loud knocking on the door. I told Mom it was the principal and not to answer the door. Mr. Vasquez kept knocking loud and he said, "Open the door, Ms. Gonzales, it is Mr. Vasquez, the principal of McDonnell Middle school, I know you and your daughter are in there. Open the door." I told Mom not to open the door, and he said-

"Ms. Gonzales, I need to take your daughter back to the school. Students are not allowed to leave school premises during school hours."

Mom opened the door and said—"Sophia told me what happened."

Mr. Vasquez said—"Your daughter Sophia left the school premises before school was let out, and McDonnell Middle School *does not* allow their students to leave during school hours, and I'm taking her back to school with me."

Mom said—"*You* are *not* taking my daughter *anywhere*. She is very upset and she is staying with me."

Mr. Vasquez insisted, but my mother was adamant and he finally left. The next day she went to the school to confront the teacher, but the teacher denied everything. My mom didn't let the situation go. She asked the principle to bring in other students who told the story exactly as I had. We made a complaint, but Mrs. Jackson was just told not to do it again and nothing more.

CHAPTER 12

The Single Wide Trailer Days

1982-1985 El Campo, Texas

In 1982, we moved to El Campo, Texas in the country. Our uncle was glad to have us move out of his house because he could make more money renting it out. He was more than happy to loan Mom $5,000.00 in order to buy an old, beat-up mobile home and put it on a trailer lot in El Campo. When Mom applied for the lot, the good 'ol boy who owned the property was quite smitten with Mom's charm and beauty, so he didn't even ask her if she was married, or how many kids she had. Next thing you know, we all moved on to his property: Mom, eight kids, and her husband.

My brother Andretti played football on the El Campo football team. One day, all the kids were playing football outside and the owner thought we were all making too much noise. He didn't like the fact that my brothers had some of their black friends over playing with us. He and his buddies had had a few too many beers and decided to start some trouble. They came down to our side and started a brawl with Francisco and his friend Jorge. One of the owner's friends picked up a long two by four and swung it around, full-force hitting Francisco right in his face, breaking his nose. Blood splattered everywhere! Francisco ran around the back of the trailer and ran inside.

Jorge got in his Torino and sped off, spitting up gravel from the driveway as he fled away. That really made the owner mad, so he ran off to his trailer to get his *guns*! Mom saw there was going to be more trouble, and she quickly gathered all the children together and had us all lay flat on the floor in the furthest back bedroom. Francisco got his gun and Mom called 911, but before she even got off the phone, shots were being fired. The trailer park owner and his buddies started shooting at our trailer. The 911 operator heard the shooting and dispatched the police.

Cops and more cops, as well as a couple of ambulances, came immediately speeding in with sirens, lights, and all. They arrived while the shooting was still going on. They handcuffed everyone, but after asking a few questions, they believed the trailer park owner when he said Francisco had started the shooting first. They released them and took him to jail. Francisco did shoot one of the owner's buddies and wounded him, he was taken to the hospital and Francisco went to jail. He was beat up pretty bad. Mom said she was actually glad he got beaten up because he deserved it and now he knew what it felt like.

Things were getting rough for the older boys at home. Francisco was pushing them around and bullying them, it was sad. He was just a stupid hateful person. This gave Mom and Francisco something else to fight about.

One morning Andretti got up really early and woke up Luigio, Sebastian Jr. and Stefano. He said;

"Hey, guys . . . wake up, get ready. We're gonna run away!"

"I don't like it here, we don't need to live with adults."

The boys got up and they didn't understand what Andretti was up to but they did what he said.

"Hurry, grab you stuff and get all your spears and bows and arrows we made. We're gonna live in the woods."

They were still half asleep. They all loaded up with everything they could carry and snuck outside. They started walking towards a wooded area.

Over the past couple weeks Andretti had been teaching them to make bows, arrows and spears. They had built up quite a collection of survival equipment. When Andretti was showing them how to make them he said they were using a special technique the Indians used when making their hunting tools. He said that the bows and arrows were strong enough to kill animals.

They walked to the woods and decided on a spot where they would take shelter. Andretti said;

"This is where we are going to live; we're going to live on the land like cowboys."

They left some of their stuff there and went walking through the woods. Andretti had a pellet gun. He told them they were going to find something to kill to eat. They took the bows, arrows and spears. They looked around for hours but they couldn't even find a rabbit or bird to kill. It was getting later in the day and they decided to spread out. After a while they still could not find anything to kill and eat.

They hooked back up, started walking until they arrived at the creek. As they walked up close to the creek they saw lots of crawfish in the water. They looked at each other and started to yell out with excitement, they were all thrilled!

Luigio said;

"Let's grab as many as we can and roll them up inside our shirts".

They tucked as many as they could in their shirts and walked back to the campout spot. Andretti and Luigio were able to start a fire and they all helped gather wood to keep the fire going. Their plan was to cook the crawfish with their fire and then eat them. They emptied their crawfish on the ground. They sat down by the fire and they looked around at each other and then at the crawfish, they were grossed out by the thought of eating those creatures.

Andretti picked up the first one and showed them how to peel the meat out of the tail and then he stuck it on a twig and cooked it over the fire. They all watched him with repulsed looks on their faces. It was a tiny piece of meat, after a couple seconds he took it off the fire and put it in his mouth and ate it. Andretti told them that they all need to eat some. Stefano started crying and said;

"I won't eat it, no I won't!"

Luigio and Sebastian Jr. both ate one. After that Andretti decided he didn't want to eat another one and told everyone that they were just going to go back home. They had been gone all day, it was starting to get dark and they were hungry. Andretti, Luigio, Sebastian Jr. and Stefano packed up their homemade survival equipment and headed back home.

For Lindsey, Emily and I one of our escapes was when our cousin Lynn would invite us to her grandmother's lake house for the weekend. On the surface Lynn looked very snobbish like some of the girls at school. She always wore gold jewelry, and knew how to fix her hair and dress so perfect. Besides, she was very pretty. Because of all that I always worried that the more time she spent with us the more likely it was that she would soon hate us. But that was completely the opposite from what happened. When she would stay at our house for the weekends, undoubtedly it was like culture shock for her. We didn't have anything to really impress her with and it was hectic and we were squeezed into a small trailer.

Ironically when she would leave after spending the weekend with us she would kiss and hug Mom and then each one of us and say;

"Thank you for having me over this weekend, I had a great time and I love you guys!"

When she took us three older girls to her grandmother's lake house we were in another world. It was truly a 24 hour party for us. We goofed off, painted our faces like beauty queens, listened to Grease and danced around the place without a care in the world. We dressed up in our bikinis and took silly pictures of each other. Right in their back yard we could swing off a rope that dropped us into the lake. We swam, laughed and didn't worry about one single thing! There were no clothes we had to wash, no kids to take care of. It was therapeutic for us, including our sweet cousin Lynn.

Francisco wasn't at home very often. He left early for work and sometimes didn't come back home for days at a time. We loved it when he wasn't around and everything seemed perfect at home. When he was home and got mad about something, his face got really red and he looked like he was going to explode. We would get scared, but then got used to it and tried hard not to laugh (he looked just like a mean, mad bull). He still would get into fights with Mom, but every time we heard them fighting we all ran to their room and busted open the door and screamed;

"STOP IT PAPA!"

For a while, things went back and forth. Francisco started going to church with us and tried to change, but it never lasted, and he would be back to his old ways: drinking, smoking pot, and blowing steam out of his nostrils. Sometimes he was happy about something and would try to be nice to us.

We had to move again (does that surprise you?). We moved to another small nearby country town. There was a beautiful lot for sale. Mom talked to the owner and told him what had happened with the shootout, and told him we had a lawsuit pending, and as soon as we won, we could give him some money toward the one-acre lot he had for sale. In the meantime, he rented us a small A-frame house, and we stayed there for several months until we won the lawsuit.

We received the money from the law suit and gave all $5,000.00 toward the purchase of the land and moved our mobile home onto the property. At first we were not used to being in the woods in a small country town. It was serene and there were lots of places we could go on trail walks. There was a creek behind our trailer that we walked to all the time. When we first moved in, it seemed like the trailer was strong enough to live in, and we were excited about our new home.

We didn't have a septic system, electricity, heat, or water. I don't understand what my mom was thinking—how did she think we could live without water, electricity, or toilets? We lived in a torn down, beaten up, old seventy-foot long, three-bedroom trailer stuck with the fork end into the ground in the middle of a heavily wooded lot.

Mom said that she was tired of trouble—of getting kicked out of apartments, and this was all we could afford. Also, no one could kick us out. We moved in, just like that. And Mom said, "No air conditioning, no heat, but it's ours!"

Mom and Lindsey got creative and dug deep holes under the toilet. They took large rubber trash cans and punched holes in the bottom of them and placed gravel in them, then slipped them into the hole under the toilet. Mom asked the neighbors if we could buy water from them, and she connected a super long garden hose from their outside faucet and carried it all the way to our house. She slipped it through the kitchen window. Later, Mom went to the local hardware store and asked a lot of questions about how to connect the water to the trailer. She figured out how to connect the hose to the makeshift toilet with the water turned on. It made the water flow through the house and we were able to flush the toilet, take baths, and wash our clothes by hand.

Eventually, we found someone to help us run the electrical conduit through the trailer and connect it to an electrical source from the power company. Wow! Little by little, we were making it a home. We were instructed that no one could poop in the bathrooms—we had to use the toilets at school, or at a friend's house. Eventually, the Church of Christ came through for us and donated and installed a septic tank.

Lindsey got a job at Kroger and worked full-time to help support us. At first, she worked as a bagger. She started a contest to see who could bag groceries the fastest and she won. She also got really good at bringing in shopping carts from the parking lot. She could bring in as many as the guys could. She was promoted to cashier and we were so proud of her. Her job at Kroger was important, and we needed the money. She liked working there and got good at checking out customers. She memorized all the right change to give people. For example, she knew that if something ended in 79 cents and the customer gave her a dollar, then they would get exactly 21 cents back.

Mom was always thinking up new projects for us to all participate in and places we would all go to enjoy together (like parks and her friend's homes to visit). Even when we didn't have much, most of the time she managed to come up with a delicious dinner that we always looked forward to at the end of our day. We helped Mom plant a garden, too. We started this project where we picked a section in the back of our trailer and called it our new garden. We had to do a lot of prep work before we could plant anything, we probably would have told Mom we didn't want a garden if we had any idea how hard it would be to get it ready to plant!

Our hard work surely paid off and we couldn't wait to go to our garden to see what new veggies popped up out of the ground. We had tomatoes, green beans, carrots, lettuce, and lots of other vegetables. Also in the area that we lived we could take walks and find areas where we could pick the wild grapes off of overgrown grape vines and Mom would make grape juice, grape syrup, and she even tried to make wine. The neighbor lady had chickens and every day she was kind enough to give us fresh eggs! Of course, as you may agree, you can't succeed without failing. We tried to grow peanuts and it was a complete disaster. We had lots of trouble getting rid of the ants that started to appear because of the peanuts.

We were enjoying the natural benefits of living in the country. When you were a kid did your mother ever say, "GO outside and play, and don't come back until dark!"?

Well our mother did. The boys did every single outside activity they could dream up. For example, Luigio thought up a "follow the leader" game. He told Andretti, Sebastian Jr. and Stefano;

"Let's play follow the leader"

"You have to jump and swing like a monkey from tree to tree. You can't touch the ground because it's *LAVA!*"

Our brothers made all kinds of creative and crafty things outside. Besides the bows, arrows and spears they made lots of different water toys to play with down by the creek; like, rafts out of milk jugs and floating boats out of braded twigs.

The longer we lived in our trailer, the more we decorated the inside. Mom played our music really loud on the weekends and we cleaned and straightened up our little mobile home. We played Dan Fogelberg, Kenny Rogers, and many other wonderful musical artists. They inspired us while we cleaned. I think listening to the music was also therapeutic and it put us in great spirits. When we listened to the radio while cleaning, Mom and us older girls each felt different emotions when certain songs were playing.

Sometimes we all started crying and other times we sang along with the songs as though we were expressing how we felt. For example, when "Goodbye To You" by Scandal would play, we sang along like we were telling off everyone who had hurt us in the past. When "Total Eclipse Of The Heart" by Bonnie Tyler played, we just broke down and cried because it made us think about Dad, and we missed him. When Michael Jackson's music came on the radio, the boys would come running in the living room to bust out their moves. We couldn't help it—we all started dancing and didn't stop until we were exhausted.

> *"May we never let the things we can't have, or don't have, or shouldn't have, spoil our enjoyment of the things we do have and can have. As we value our happiness, let us not forget it, for one of the greatest lessons in life is learning to be happy without the things we cannot or should not have."*
> *—Richard L. Evans*

Our front yard was all dirt and trees, so there wasn't much we could do to make it pretty. We made a fence next to the trailer where we started to add different kinds of animals. It wasn't my idea. I was so busy with cleaning the kitchen and helping out with laundry that I didn't think we needed all those animals to take care of. It seemed like other people thought we needed animals though, because friends kept giving them to us, and Mom didn't have the heart to ever say no.

Someone gave us a pony and we named her Alisha. Another person gave us a baby goat, which needed to be bottle-fed. We named our baby goat *Shusham*. People also gave us puppies, kittens, ducks, and chickens! We took care of every one of them for as long as we lived there, which wasn't very long. We had a tragedy with our pony, the school bus hit her and the sheriff had to come out and shoot her. We were all devastated.

We didn't have a washing machine, but when we could afford to, we took the laundry to a Laundromat. When we went to the Laundromat we camped out there for the entire day, it was so unbelievably boring for us! Most of the time, we washed our clothes by hand. We put the dirty clothes in the bathtub, rolled up our pants, poured in some soap, and stomped the clothes really fast. Then we drained the water and rinsed them, rang them outside, and hung them on the clothesline.

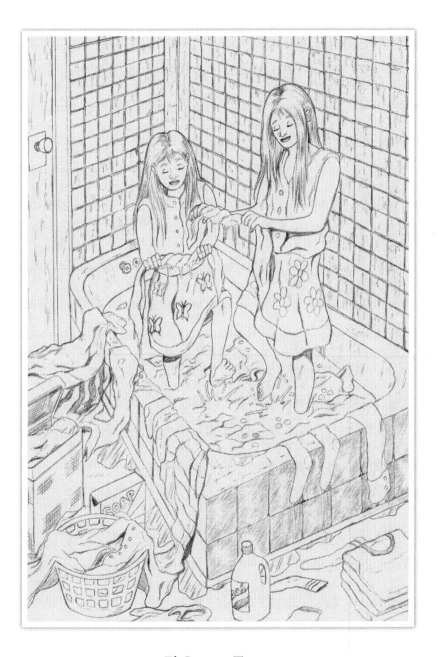

El Campo, Texas.
Emily and Sophia washing clothes their bath tub.

1983 El Campo

Mom became pregnant with baby number nine. The trailer only had three bedrooms, and the four girls slept on one full-sized bed that was at the end of one side of the trailer. My four brothers slept in a room with one set of bunk beds, and sometimes they preferred to sleep on the floor so they could sprawl out. The summer was very uncomfortable. In the girls' room, Lindsey, Emily, Madeline, and I squeezed into one bed, and we were sweaty and sticky all night. I also hated the buzzing sound of the mosquitoes at night. When it got really bad, Mom would load us all up in our 1960s orange Volkswagen van, which had air conditioning. She used to let us cool off and sleep while she drove around.

Mom had her total breakdowns. Sometimes late at night we could hear her crying herself to sleep. At times she probably lost her mind and felt trapped with all of us. All we could do was let her know we loved her.

There was a nearby neighborhood swimming pool that had not been used or taken care of for many years. Inside the pool it had accumulated lots of weeds and trash and it also had snakes. Our family got together with all the kids in the neighborhood and made a plan to clean up the pool so we could all use it. It was a huge success. All the kids in our area got together, the parents served hot dogs, chips and sodas for all the "little helpers". The adults brought gallons of bleach, and used the nearby neighbor's hoses and brooms to scrub the big old filthy pool. Eventually it got clean and everyone went swimming. After that we all had an awesome pool party.

It was August of 1983 and a Hurricane named Alicia was headed for Texas.

"Hurricane Alicia was the first named storm and first hurricane of the 1983 Atlantic hurricane season. Alicia was the season's strongest and deadliest storm of the season, while killing a total of 21 people and causing $2.6 billion (1983 dollars) in damage. Alicia was the most destructive Texas hurricane since Hurricane Carla from 1961" (by Simple English Wikipedia).

As news came that the hurricane was headed straight towards our town, a neighbor who owned an old vacant concrete block house, allowed us to stay there during the hurricane. We were all terrified and huddled together, praying as the hurricane roared and the eye hovered directly over us...in a very still frightening moment it passed over us, ripping trees out of the ground and debris flying all around us. There was no electricity, or running water, but we had prepared and filled containers of water, made sandwiches, had instant soups, had candles, blankets and a first aid kit.

When the storm was over, and we left the house, we found our trailer had shifted and was leaning over, a large tree had fallen on it and made a huge dent, but it was not destroyed. The Church of Christ sent members over to help clean up the mess and remove the tree from off the trailer. We gave them sandwiches and lemonade and all worked together. Then we moved back in our home.

In the winter we were very cold, but Mom always opened the oven and turned it on for us early in the morning. When it was freezing, Mom left the oven on all night for us. The Church of Christ came through for us again and gave us a kerosene space heater, which helped a great deal. Mom hung blankets from floor to ceiling to separate the hallway from the living room in order to contain the heat. We all slept on the living room floor cuddled up together to keep warm.

Clothes would take days to dry on the clothesline, so we spread out the wet, clean clothes all over the kitchen and living room to dry. After I washed my jeans, I often had to wear them to school while they were still wet. I tried not to let kids sit too close to me on the bus because they would think that it was weird for me to be wearing wet clothes. Once I got to school, my jeans would dry by about second period and I wouldn't have to worry about it anymore.

Lindsey and I were really different teenagers. She dropped out of ninth grade to work full-time to help support the family. Lindsey took on a fatherly role and deep down inside Mom was happy when she decided to quit high school and work full-time.

123

I stayed in school and worked part-time in a Mexican restaurant. There were so many neat things I learned at that restaurant. I was surprised by the recipe for refried beans. They cooked beans with equal parts beans and lard. It was impressive to see how many times they could reheat flour tortillas by just running them under water and then re-cooking them in the skillet.

We always had trailer construction projects going on. I guess we made a little progress with all the sweat equity we put into them, but it really didn't make much difference. I noticed a lot of things about the trailer that always bothered me. I don't know why, but it was as if I thought everything should be seamless and new. There were tiny little holes in the floor where you could see the ground, and there were cracks in the front and back door where you could also see outside. There were bullet holes in the sides of the trailer from the shootout.

The window screens were torn. The linoleum floors were curling up at the edges, and there were so many more bits and pieces of imperfection that just added to my aggravation. I was beginning to really wish we had a nicer home. If we didn't keep the trailer really clean, there would be roaches all over the place. Those were the only creatures that were brave enough to come out when we were around. But even though our kitchen was spotless and smelled strongly like Pine-Sol, there was nothing we could do about the roaches falling out of the kitchen cabinets when we opened the doors (this old trailer was infested with roaches when we got it).

We finally had consistency and stability in our lives, and that was a great feeling for all of us. Mom held our regular family meetings. She always talked what was going on that week in our home and the problems we were having and that agenda item would end with a plan to fix the problem. Sometimes she would cry and other times one of us kids would start crying and talking about our problems. Before our family meeting were over mom would start to tell cute stories about each of us, and we would all start laughing. After the family meetings it would usually lead us into doing something fun together like making popcorn or playing music (of course playing music sometimes lead us to doing other fun things like watching one of my brothers' break dance or someone acting silly and all of us laughing at them).

All us big girls (including Mom) would chase the boys and our baby girl all around the trailer. We were pretty rough on the trailer. My brothers would run around and smash into the walls. Mom wanted to make the boys' bedroom larger, so she took a hammer and tore down the wall dividing their room from the hall. That gave the boys an extra three feet of space. We had to walk through their room to get to our room, but that was okay. Mom put a second set of bunk beds in the boys' room so they each had their own beds now.

We would all run around with excitement, screaming and laughing, and by the time we stopped we had huge smiles on our faces and were ready to go to sleep. The boys were very spoiled, not materially, but because we were taught to treat men differently and to wait on them, which is what we did. That's how Mom was raised, and she also learned the same in the cult, so she carried the tradition on with our family.

We adored our little brothers; they were like our little children. We would give them foot massages and tickle their backs at night until they fell asleep. As they got older, they were very loving to us too, and would rub our feet when we came home tired and late from work. Today our brothers are still happy to give us shoulder and foot massages—all we have to do is ask.

When mom was eight months pregnant with Annabelle, Lindsey had just quit her job because her boss was always making advances toward her. Mom and Lindsey drove around looking for a new job for Lindsey. They drove to a nearby gun store and decided to stop there. Lindsey walked in and asked if she could work there. The owner had just accidentally shot himself in the leg and his eighteen-year-old son was working in the store. He said, "Yes, you can work here and we'll pay you $3.00 an hour."

Mom would drop Lindsey off at the gun shop and pick her up. She first started cleaning the store and cleaning the guns with window cleaner.

Lindsey didn't know anything about guns, but she was a quick learner, and the owner's son started to teach her. She started to learn about all different kinds of guns, and the owners let her practice shooting targets outside the store. She was a straight shooter. She worked there for a couple weeks, and when she asked for her paycheck, they said they didn't have any money to pay her.

When mom picked Lindsey up after work, she told her what they said and Mom told her to go right back in the store and tell them to give her a gun since they couldn't pay her. Mom and Lindsey took the gun to a pawn shop and got $40 for it. Then they went to the Sack-N-Save and bought $40 worth of groceries. Even though she was not paid cash, she returned to work anyway.

Lindsey learned how to manually reload bullets for the guns used for target practice by the El Campo police department. The police brought in boxes of bullets, hundreds at once. One at a time, she took the primer out of the shell, put a new primer in, put gun powder in, then a lead slug, and crimped it shut. She got really good at it and the gun shop owner started to give her guns for payment, which she sold. The police were regular customers and one day they dropped off fifty boxes of empty shells and said that they needed them reloaded in a hurry for their classes.

She had started to reload them when a drunken man walked in the store. He saw what she was doing and told her that he could do it faster than she could. He came behind the counter and while she was putting a shell in the re-loader with her right hand to pop the primer out, he put his hand on the handle and pulled it all the way down. The reloading die that was supposed to go through the bullet to pop out the primer went through her finger and then through the bullet. When he saw what he had done, he let go and ran out of the store.

Lindsey's finger was still stuck in the reloading machine and bleeding bad. She had to raise the handle to release the die and get her finger out. She walked outside to look for help and a police car had just pulled up; when the officer saw her, he took her to the hospital. She had surgery on her finger and stayed in the hospital for days. For over ten years her finger was badly disfigured. We all used to say that she had an "E.T." finger, because that is what it looked like.

1984 El Campo, Texas

Precious baby **Annabelle** was born. She was the cutest, most adorable baby with very dark hair with tight curls. We had so much fun with her. Most of the time, she slept with Mom but still slept with us in the girls room often. We were happy there even though we had a very small kitchen, very small bedrooms, and a very small bathroom. Even the front and back doors were small and it was really hard to get furniture through them. We were determined to make it as nice as possible. Mom went to every charitable furniture drop box she could find, as often as she could. Today Mom gives back—she is always donating and giving to charities and needy families.

The trailer wasn't as sturdy as we thought. Sometimes when we were all piled up in the girls' room, we would forget that the trailer wasn't leveled and bolted down to the ground, and it would start to tilt. We all felt the trailer tilt downwards and we all looked at each other in complete shock and Mom started screaming, "Hurry boys . . . run to the other side! Hurry boys! Go . . . run before it tilts over!" Then we all started screaming for them to hurry. My little brothers were like four little lightning bolts, and they were yelling at each other to run faster. When they ran to the other side of the trailer, we felt it level out.

Our trailer inside was so nice that I wanted to do something about the front yard too. Mom always said that if you tend to your garden, it will bear fruit. So, I volunteered to mow the leaves and ground even though we just had tiny patches of grass. I thought if I mowed the dirt, grass would grow. We had an old lawn mower, but we never used it and it was always out of gas. The church donated some sod, and we planted the grass in front of our trailer. Mom hung up a swing from a big, old tree. One night, she snuck away with the boys. They had found an abandoned field with a big pile of bricks in it. Mom and my little brothers loaded up the bricks in the back of the car and brought them home. That was our next weekend's project, to create a cute, little winding path with the bricks in front of our trailer. I love looking at those pictures of my small brothers in the front yard carrying grass pallets when we were working on our yard projects.

One day, I was really anxious to mow and the lawn mower would not start because it was out of gas. I knew exactly what to do because we used to run out of gas a lot when we were traveling. I found the hose, cut a piece off, and put one end of it in the gas tank of our car and started to inhale really hard on the other end to get the gas to come out. I kept sucking real hard, but the hose was too long and nothing was coming out. I prayed and tried it again and gasoline came gushing out, and I accidently swallowed some gasoline. I ran in the house and Mom, not knowing what to do, just prayed frantically over me and took me to the neighbors for help. Each neighbor lady had a different solution. One had me eat a bunch of bread and another had me drink cooking oil. I told Mom I still didn't feel good, but I wanted to go home. I never did that again!

One time when Annabelle was a baby we all went to the beach in our VW van. When it was time to leave, we got back in our van to go home, and as we were driving off Mom said-

"Okay, time for roll call. Lindsey, Sophia, Emily, Andretti, Luigio, Sebastian Jr., Stefano, Madeline," and everyone said here except for Madeline. Mom said-

"Madeline"

"Madeline is not in the car!"

"That's not funny."

"No," "Really, she is not in the car." Mom screamed and turned the car around. We saw a police car and we flagged him down. Most of us got out and told him what happened and he followed us back to the beach. When we got there, Madeline was playing in the sand and hadn't even noticed we had left.

To be honest, this wasn't the first time this happened. A while back when Stefano was just learning to talk we all went to the movies. When we were leaving the movie theatre in our VW van Stefano was yelling "Mommy, Mommy" and no one really knew what was going on. We looked at him and he had a scared little look on his face. Then we saw out the window of the car that Sebastian Jr. was running as fast as his short legs could move him yelling and trying to catch up with our car. We didn't do roll call that time, otherwise we probably wouldn't have left him behind.

**Elizabeth driving away in the VW van after a movie
leaving Sebastian Jr. behind.**

One day in eleventh grade, everyone was talking about college and I was very confused about what it was; I wondered why I had never heard about it before. When I got home I asked Mom to explain college to me. She said, "Honey, college is a place that some kids go to after high school to continue their education that is very far away and costs a lot of money." I told her I wanted to go to college and she said, "Oh honey, you can't. We can't afford that, and I need you here to help with the family." She really didn't want me to go to college because she felt like she needed my help with the kids. I didn't talk to her about it again, but I still was planning on finding out how I could go.

Mom and Lindsey often worked as a team. Mom was the leader and we called Lindsey "The Boss." They were practical and had good knee-jerk reactions. We were in our small kitchen one evening eating dinner, and Mom saw a large snake sliver out of the kitchen utensil drawer. She gasped for air and yelled, "Nobody move! There's a huge snake in the kitchen drawer." It was literally hanging over the edge of the drawer about fifteen inches. We all looked at Mom then looked around at each other as if the end-time had come. She said-

"Quick, Lindsey, grab your gun and *kill that snake.*"

Instantly Lindsey, the straight shooter she was, took her Smith & Wesson in hand and aimed at the snake. She shot and killed it, then proceeded to grab the dead snake and throw it in the wooded lot behind our house. We were relieved, but we never did anything about the huge hole in the drawer and floor from the bullets. I didn't pay much attention at the time, but I found out later that the gun shop owner had given Lindsey a lot of other guns because he could never pay her in cash. He also, paid her one month by giving her a window unit air conditioner, which proved to be the greatest of all payments.

We put it in the girls' room that summer and at least we were cool and comfortable for a while during the horrible, hot days. It wasn't long before someone figured out that the boys should sleep in there too!

Emily was always the early bird, so she had enough time in the morning to do what she needed to get ready. Emily wasn't really a cooking and cleaning kind of girl like Lindsey and I, but she noticed other important things that needed to be done and made sure that she took care of them. Every morning she got up early and made a fresh pot of coffee. She poured a tall cup for Mom and woke her with it each morning. We all joked about it because Mom loved having her coffee served to her in the morning, and it helped her get out of bed because she didn't want her coffee to get cold.

While Lindsey and I catered mostly to our little brothers, Emily loved our baby sisters Madeline and Annabelle and took really good care of them. We all had so much fun with our baby sisters. Emily would fix their hair and make or find cute little girly things to dress them up with. We liked seeing them prance around looking just as cute as they could be. Homework was really important to Emily, and she did it every day. She also remembered to take it with her when she left for the bus stop. I guess that is why she always made really good grades in school.

Since Emily got up so early in the mornings and was always ready for school before the bus came, it was her job to go to the bus stop and scream "THE BUS" when she saw it coming. She had to scream it loud enough for us to hear it from the trailer. Also, she knew she wasn't allowed to get completely on the bus because if she did, it would drive off without all of us, so she would put one foot on the step to the bus, and one on the street, pretending to buckle or tie her shoes. The bus driver knew what she was doing but let her do it anyway.

She left to walk to the bus stop while Lindsey, Mom, and I were inside trying to get the boys up and ready. We woke up the four boys and I started tickling their backs and saying-

"Wake up little brothers," then five minutes later I walked back in-

"Okay, this is the second time. Wake up, or you'll be late for school."

Ten minutes later I went back in and started cursing at them. Emily was at the bus stop and we heard her screaming-

"THE BUS, THE BUS, THE BUS!!!"

When the boys heard Emily's scream, they got up, grabbed their shirt and shoes, and ran out the front door. When we first moved on that property, we didn't have any steps that led into the trailer by the front door, so we had to step on an upside down bucket. When the boys were in a hurry to run out of the trailer to catch the bus they missed the bucket and fell to the ground but quickly got right back up and kept running. Sometimes when we stepped on the bucket it fell over and we still fell on the ground, it was just another aggravation to our daily morning routine (we were always in such a hurry to get out the door). Eventually, a neighbor who went to our church made us a set of wooden steps, and it was much nicer and easier to get in and out of the house.

On our way getting off to the bus stop there was a long driveway that we had to run down and by the time we got on the bus we could hardly breathe from running so fast. I got so frustrated because it seemed like I spent all my time waking up the boys, and I didn't have time to even get myself ready. What was worse—the boys didn't even want to go to school, but I really wanted to make it to school and stay in school.

Our little animals loved us! As we all ran down our driveway to get on the bus, Shusham (our pet goat) and our rooster ran after us. So we all ran to the bus stop and got on the school bus, including *Shusham and Mr. Rooster.* Our bus driver was already mad at us all and now we had to catch Shusham and the rooster and throw them off the bus. We asked our bus driver if we could take them back home real quick but she didn't even answer and gave us a very scary mean face. It was so embarrassing because right away Shusham pooped everywhere, and it was almost impossible to get him off the bus! The rooster was easy to catch. Our bus driver looked at us every morning when she opened the bus door like she totally hated our family.

El Campo, Texas. Sophia, Emily, Andretti, Luigio, Sebastian and Stefano running to catch the school bus. Family Goat is also in line to hop on bus.

When I was about fourteen, a boy invited me to the movies. I remember asking my mother if I could go and she said, "Sure you can, as long as you take all your brothers and Emily." It wouldn't be fair if I went and they had to stay home. By that time, Mom had a certain kind of insanity about her, but she was so overwhelmed with all of us. I was mad because I knew the boy wouldn't pay for all of us, and even if he had, he wouldn't want to take all those kids with him to the movies.

I told my friend I had to take all my brothers and my sister, and I could not believe it when he said that was okay. He said he drove a station wagon, so he had plenty of room for everyone. I remember sitting in the theater holding my youngest brother in my arms and feeling so embarrassed. The boy tried to talk to me, but I was too busy with my brothers to talk to him. I felt that it was so unfair that Mom made me take my brothers and sister on my first date.

We became very settled in our little trailer, but we still had a tough time. Mom was financially creative. She baked delicious cheesecakes and pies to sell to the neighbors. Great-Uncle Bob came over to visit often and brought us groceries once a week. He brought milk, bread, and eggs, and sometimes ice cream and cookies!

During Christmas, we had so much food on the table that it was unbelievable! Mom made fresh apple pies, pecan pies, cheesecake, homemade stuffing, homemade bread, and so much more. We told her how much we loved her food, and she just kept making more and more to put on the table every year. She was probably trying to make up for all the years we did not have Christmas.

Christmas was so much fun. It seemed like everyone who knew about our family wanted to bring us presents. We had presents from the Mormons, presents from the neighbors, presents from Uncle Bob, and presents from the little chapel we went to in town, gifts from Mom and gifts from Lindsey, Emily, and me for our younger siblings.

Every Christmas Eve, Mom had a bad habit of pacing around and feeling like she didn't get us enough presents. She would tell Lindsey and me that she felt bad because she still wanted more presents under the tree. She ran out late to buy more presents and would be gone for hours. She really didn't need to do that. She would come back with huge bags of dollar store gifts and we would stay up drinking hot chocolate and eating Christmas cookies while we helped her wrap them all. A family a few doors down from ours had two little boys, and their family was worse off than ours. These two boys started coming to our house every day to eat. During Christmas, Mom made sure there was enough food and gifts for them.

We were going to a Bible chapel at the time, and the members knew about our family and our financial situation. The elderly members of the church donated some of their dresses and other clothes to us, and Mom, Lindsey, Emily, and I started wearing them to church.

Mom decided to open a resale shop and clothing boutique in an old hundred year old house. Uncle Bob provided us with the money to rent the building ($150 a month) and bought us paint. Mom painted the inside of the house and drew a picture of a corset with a big petticoat under it on a large piece of wood and wrote "Petticoat Junction" in huge letters.

The first week we opened, Mom had several orders for prom dresses. Of course she was very happy and motivated to stay up several nights to finish them. With the leftover fabric, she made Lindsey, Emily, Madeline, Annabelle, and me Easter dresses. They were precious. She made the boys vests. Lindsey, being the sharpest tool in our shed, remembers *exactly* what the dresses looked like. Mom took all the different pieces of fabric and cut them into pie-shaped triangles and sewed them together. The dresses were so full that they flared out when we walked.

We showed up at church on Easter Sunday elegantly dressed in our *designer* dresses. It gave us such a sense of pride, self-worth, and beauty. At church everyone noticed we were wearing new dresses, and they complimented us the whole time we were there. We also got extra attention from the cute boys at church.

These dresses gained Mom a reputation as a brilliant seamstress, and so mothers started calling her at the boutique to place more orders for their daughters' prom dresses. Lindsey also helped her make them. It was an exhilarating and exciting experience to be asked to make and create all those beautiful dresses. Mom made some of the dresses without patterns; she got creative and made them however she wanted.

For my prom, Mom sewed me a lovely red and white southern dress and helped Lindsey make her own beautiful lacy purple dress. Lindsey wasn't going to school, but Mom said that she could go with me to the prom anyway. Lindsey could drive, and I needed someone to take me.

We were excited about going and showing off our dresses. Wonderful Uncle Bob came over to take pictures (**present day**, we still have these pictures of Lindsey and I just before prom in our Southern dresses). We were so proud of Petticoat Junction that we took our prom pictures in the boutique. Mom also took several pictures of Uncle Bob and I. Lindsey and I also took one together at the prom.

When we arrived at prom and walked in the ballroom I was very nervous because I didn't know what style everyone else was wearing. But I was still excited about my beautiful dress. We were surprised when we saw lots of girls wearing dresses similar to ours: long and very full.

All the kids were into Michael Jackson and Break-dancing. We wanted the store to attract as many people as possible, so we stocked up on Michael Jackson costumes, hats, gloves, belts, posters and other accessories. We all loved going there and playing with all that cool stuff. The only problem was the kids in the neighborhood couldn't afford them, so we ended up giving most of them away.

Mom and Lindsey worked hard to sell the clothes they made and keep the business, but there weren't enough customers in that tiny town to keep Petticoat Junction open. Sadly, we were forced to close it down.

> *Yesterday's failures must be forgotten. Tomorrow's new hope*
> *and new fulfillment must be cherished.*
> —*Sri Chinmoy*[26]

Just before we closed down Petticoat Junction mom had been very active in a movement to stop schools from beating or "popping" children in school. The local schools used corporal punishment (spankings with a wooden paddle) as discipline. Parents had to sign an agreement to give them this right. Mom refused to sign the agreement, but they popped us anyway.

Mom was very out spoken and protective of us all. My brothers were always getting into trouble in school, if they were sent to the principal's office she would be there to defend them.

One day Andretti came home with markings and bruises up and down his butt and the backs of his legs. Mom was furious! She was at the school the next morning screaming at the school administration, waving polaroid pictures that she took of him. She threatened them in every way she knew how including reporting them to the police and the news.

So, just before we closed the store, the TV news station came out to Petticoat Junction to interview her about how the school took advantage of abusing and beating the children. Shortly after that, the schools had to change their policy and no longer use that method of punishment. (For years to come, our younger brothers would tell us that their teachers would still threaten them with pops and would get very upset when they would respond saying they couldn't pop them anymore.)

For a short while, Mom got a job cleaning a truck stop. It was very filthy, but she took pride in trying her best to keep it as clean as she could. Lindsey and I went to work with her. We didn't like to go because we had to be there to clean at 4:00 in the morning. We earned $50.00 a week. Thankfully, for Lindsey and I Mom got fired and we didn't have to work

---

[26] Chinmoy Kumar Ghose, also known as Sri Chinmoy (August 27, 1931-October 11, 2007) was an Indian spiritual teacher, poet, artist and athlete.

there anymore. But Mom took it really hard; we needed the fifty dollars a week to help with the groceries (food stamps were never enough). She had been taking packets of hot chocolate and coffee without permission, and she lost her job because of it. They humiliated her and made her feel really bad about it. She cried so hard and felt horrible.

Andretti was the leader of the pack. The younger three brothers would follow him around everywhere he allowed them to. He was like Lindsey— he had a natural instinct to lead and knew exactly what he wanted to do. He decided that he wanted to form a break dancing group with the brothers, so they all started to practice break dancing every day! They were practicing everywhere they could. When they were home, they would practice in our small kitchen floor.

We loved to watch kung fu movies. They were always on TV in the early to mid 1980s. Andretti showed us everything he learned. After the movie was over, all of us watched Andretti do kung fu and we all started doing our own version of kung fu. We came up with things to do that were so funny that some of us actually wet our pants laughing (but I won't mention who).

Andretti got behind Luigio and put his fingers on each side of Luigio's eyes and pulled them to imitate a Chinese man. Luigio would move his mouth like he was talking. Since he was the only one in our family with very dark hair, the part fit him. He would put an exaggerated mean look on his face. Andretti was hiding behind Luigio's head and he would talk exactly like they did in the kung fu movies. For example with a loud awkward choppy voice he would say, "I am kung fu master and I will defeat you, weak one. You will die." Luigio had a serious ninja look and posture and moved his arms and hands while he was acting like he was talking. When we get together now, we always make them do this because it's still as funny as it was over twenty years ago.

They were creative and got really good at being little actors. In high school, all my brothers were in theater. Anytime we were at someone's house, they would perform and got lots of attention. We loved to watch them perform, and it made things really fun at home. On the weekends we popped gigantic bowls of popcorn on the stove and poured on lots of melted butter, added salt, and stirred it up real good. We all huddled in the small living room, ate popcorn, and watched TV.

We wolfed down the popcorn and afterwards we were covered in butter and salt from our fingers to our elbows. Then we all started licking the butter off our hands. In the winter, Mom made us hot chocolate and homemade oatmeal raisin cookies. She said they were good for us because they had real oats and raisins in them, and we would curl up on blankets to watch TV.

Sebastian Jr. was Mom's little helper. He took time away from hanging out with Andretti and the boys to help Mom around the house. He helped her pick up toys and laundry off the floor. He followed her around with the cutest smile on his face (he knew he was a great little helper).

Stefano was Mommy's boy and was always picking flowers for Mommy. One day, when he was about five years old, Mom saw him picking flowers before school. She assumed they were for her and said, "Oh you're so sweet honey, thank you." And he said, "Sorry Mommy, these are for my girlfriend, but don't be sad because I still love you." He always had a tender heart. Several years later, Stefano became a fix-it-up handyman kid. He was always wanted to take something apart or break it so he could fix it and put it back together again.

One night Francisco was very drunk. We were on guard; he already knew he was outnumbered. We started to hear furniture move around and knew that he and Mom were fighting again. Immediately we ran to the living room to break up the fight. We were all crowded together and looked at Francisco. His eyes were bloodshot and he looked pitiful! We looked at Mom and were shocked by the look on her face. She had a lamp in her hand and was about to throw it at Francisco—she was beyond mad. She was out-of-control-pissed-off and fighting back!

She told us to leave and go to our rooms. She swung the heavy lamp at him and he fell limp to the floor. Not knowing if he would get up and start beating on her again, she pushed him out the front door and he toppled down the wooden steps to the ground. She called us and told us to quickly go out the back door. It was about 3:00 a.m. and all nine of us kids and Mom walked down the country road to a neighbor's house. Unfortunately our cousin Lynn was with us that night and she had to suffer through it with us. But I guess she already knew our life was chaotic and that Francisco was a bad person.

The neighbors called the police, and when they arrived they saw that mom's lip was bleeding from the fight. Mom told the police what happened and started crying. Then said,

"I think he is dead."

She was tired and so emotionally drained. The police left a female officer with us and two male officers walked down the long driveway until they reached the trailer. Francisco was gone, nowhere to be found! The police said he probably heard the sirens and left.

Shortly after this we all moved out of our trailer and far away from Francisco and Mom divorced him.

> *Hope abides; therefore I abide. Countless frustrations have not cowed me. I am still alive, vibrant with life. The black cloud will disappear. The morning sun will appear once again in all its supernal glory.*
> *—Sri Chinmoy*

CHAPTER 13

Embracing Stability

1985 Dallas, Texas

We had lived the last couple decades in poverty but with perseverance to survive and overcome the course of events. We spent the last ten years struggling with our reintegration into society and undoing the cult's brainwashing. We had to figure out how to make enough money to pay the rent. We were forced to adjust, adapt, and survive on so many different levels: socially, emotionally, and financially.

> *"Hope is not a momentary flicker. Hope is Eternity's slow, steady, Illumining and fulfilling height."*
>
> —*Sri Chinmoy*

Family Photo of Elizabeth and children taken in 1985.
They took their first professional family portrait
to remind them of their new beginning!

A Real Woman By Lindsey Star
(written about Elizabeth-1984)

Have you ever know a real woman?
Heart of rubies, soul of passion . . .
Let me tell you about this woman I love
She is a woman of many qualities,
She's a woman who's never hard to please
Her life is worth, it's worth more than gold,
Stories of here have many times been told
She has carried 9 children next to her heart,
That she'll love forever and they'll never part
She has planned and provided and made them a life
She's fought and struggled and taught them how to survive
She's a mother and a father and a teacher in one
When things got down, she said look toward the sun
And we did . . . .
And we lived

Before we moved out of our trailer Mom had called our great aunt who lived in a beautiful part of town and told her about the things that were going on in our life. Aunt Martha helped mom put together a plan. The timing was right! Lindsey was working full-time, I was working part-time, and Mom was making money sewing a variety of fabric designs and selling baked goodies. To make money she also went to garage sales and bought clothes to resell. She took the clothes home and replaced the buttons and fixed them up nice then resold them at garage sales. At the garage sales she also sold fresh tacos, sandwiches, and cokes. Soon we had enough money to put down a deposit and first month's rent on a beautiful home just a few miles away from Aunt Martha. The home was in a beautiful neighborhood and had good schools.

Aunt Martha was very helpful in preparing Mom for the new home rental interview. She let Mom drive her beautiful new blue Cadillac and dressed Mom in her lovely designer clothes, pantyhose, and high heels. Mom looked professional, and she played the part! Aunt Martha vouched for Mom's employment reference as a home interior designer. It all happened so quickly, Mom was shocked when the landlord handed her the signed lease agreement and gave her the keys!

We all moved into this beautiful four-bedroom house in a beautiful part of Dallas Texas.

We were very excited and happy about our new home. Thankfully Francisco was finally out of the picture. We couldn't help to think of Dad, we missed him badly and in some strange way wished he was part of our family. For us older kids, we had been strongly influenced by him from back when we all lived together in Mexico. At that time there were weeks at a time when we spent twenty-four hours a day with Dad. Lindsey, Emily, Andretti, and I were real close to him and loved him very much. It was unbearable and unbelievable when we all realized that he was gone. It had been over five years since we had seen him.

Lindsey got a good job working as a cashier in a medical clinic. She worked there for a while then was offered another job working for a neurologist.

We all knew she had a great job in the medical field, but when she started working for the doctor's office we were confused about what she was doing and thought she had become a doctor. Lindsey started laughing when our brothers told her, "Wow, you're a doctor now?" Her position at the doctor's office was in the billing group. She learned her job quickly and was good at what she did, but she still had a few major things to learn. She started out typing the envelopes to patients with their name and address all on the same line. She didn't know how to spell cities and states, so she had to learn that too. I remember visiting her at her office, and I was so proud of her. Everyone at work loved her. Lindsey had learned all about the patients and could find their charts quickly. She knew what medications they were on and who their pharmacist was. I also got to meet the doctors she worked for, and they were very nice.

It was Christmas time again and many of us had jobs, it was important to us to get gifts for each other to show our love and appreciation. We have a family video from 1986 of our Christmas together. We were living in our beautiful rented home and in the Christmas video we were handing presents to each other and talking about the gifts we bought. The huge living room had wrapping paper everywhere and everyone was opening presents. We were all talking at the same time with laughter and smiley faces during the whole video. The Christmas tree was in the corner, but presents were scattered all around the floor, and the gift opening process took what seemed like forever because Mom wanted everyone to show each other what they had received and thank that person personally as they opened the gifts. **Present day**, we love watching this video. It reminds us how close we were and how we shared our life together with a great sense of care for each other.

By this time years had passed since Dad left and we had not received any phone calls, letters, or child support from Dad. We used to want our parents to get back together, but now, even though we wished we could see him, we did not want to have to live according to his beliefs. Since mom was single, we felt more comfortable talking about whatever we wanted.

This was such an exciting time, with just Mom and us nine kids, and it was so much fun living without Francisco. Lindsey had plans to get her

GED and bought a new car. I was a senior at Miranda Senior High and was excited about being a professional businesswoman after I graduated.

Mom sewed beautiful things for Aunt Martha and some of Aunt Martha's neighbors and friends as well. She wanted us to keep our new home and worked hard day and night with her interior decorating. She was doing residential work and became very good at it. She had been sewing ever since she started having children, so it was easy for her to turn her knowledge into a full-time career. She built up a clientele and was well-liked in the community. Her work was unique and well done. She took a few classes at the local community college to learn more about interior design.

The boys were in all types of sports: baseball, football, soccer, and swimming. Mom, Lindsey and I did our best to help them attend their sports events but it was very tough with our schedules and transportation situation.

They knew they had to count on some of their friends Dads to make some of their sports activities. For example, at their practices my brothers would go up to their friends Dads and say;

"Hi Mr. Watson, I am on the team, my name is Stefano and I am your son George's best friend. Can you please pick me up at my house to take me to our next football game?"

They loved to ride their bikes in the neighborhood and skateboard. We were all becoming self-established and educated. We were learning how to succeed.

> **"Great people are those who can make others feel that they, too, can become great."—Mark Twain**[27]

Andretti was an amazing kid but he was also a dangerous kid. He had broken his arm skate boarding and had been in a cast. He was 12 at the

---

[27] Samuel Langhorne Clemens (November 30, 1835-April 21, 1910), better known by his pen name Mark Twain

time, and a friend had taken a city transportation bus to his doctor's appointment to get the cast removed from his arm. Mom was working at home sewing draperies for a client; she suddenly had a sixth sense that something was wrong, so she got up from the sewing table and walked towards the door. As soon as she reached the front door, someone was banging on the door, and she instantly said; "where is he, where is my son?" He could hardly breathe as he choked out the words, "he's lying in the street, and he got hit by a car..." Mom took off running as fast as she could 2 blocks away on a major road, where she worked her way through a huge crowd of people, to find her son in a bloody mess in the middle of the road. Ambulances, the fire department, and policed cars surrounded the area. Mom approached Andretti, not knowing if he was dead or alive, crying and screaming,

"my son, honey are you alright?" He said;

"Mom, don't cause a scene!"

The ambulance took him to the hospital, with mom in tote. We were all in the waiting room praying for hours. He had broken his arm again, the other forearm, his leg, ribs, collar bone, jaw bone, fractured skull, and was in a ""body cast". Andretti spent the next few days in the hospital and then came home.

1988-1994 Dallas, Texas

We talked about Dad more and more and wished he was around. We wished we could see him but didn't want to look for him because he wasn't looking for us. Lindsey started writing poems about him. Her first poem was written in 1988.

Lindsey's poems written about dad:

1988

"We have been below poverty,
but we have always been fed.
We have been without a home,
but we always had a bed.
One person was there to wipe away the tears.
She loved us and helped us get over our fears.
She held up the fort and pulled us all through.
Mom did the job you were supposed to do.
One person was always there,
but it was never you."

1994

"Where is my Daddy?"
She would often hear,
from wondering little faces standing so near.
I don't really know,
and I can't explain but he's gone
away and life is full of change.
But will he be back?
I thought that he cared.
Please tell me Mommy,
now I'm getting scared.
Maybe it's my fault,
I did something wrong.
Well, I'm sorry but he is still gone.
No Daddy to love us,
tickle and chase us,
our daddy has left us and tried to erase us.

(See appendices for more poems.)

I was going to community college at night and working during the day. I earned enough credit hours to transfer to my college of choice, Texas Tech University.

When I started my college career I was pretty stubborn and naive. Even though I had enough hours to transfer to Texas Tech Mom told me that I wasn't ready. I thought to myself "she might be right but if I don't go to a college town and stay on campus now *I'll be too old next year to go*. So I made up my mind to go (finally got to use two scholarships I received in high school). Then, I packed up and made the exciting adventure to college.

> *Life is either a daring adventure or nothing. Security does not exist*
> *in nature, nor do the children of men as a whole experience it.*
> *Avoiding danger is no safer in the long run than exposure*[28].
> **—Helen Keller**

I missed the orientation and when I got to my dorm all the other girls were settled into their dorms. This was my new adventure and I was scared that college would be too hard for me but I felt like *that was okay* because I was just very happy to actually be there. I had been dreaming about it ever since that day I heard the kids talk about it in 11th grade. When I figured out that I can stay there a whole school year even if I failed the first semester then I felt much better about the whole thing.

My dorm building was huge and it took me a couple days to feel comfortable wondering around and being able to find my way back to my room. Finding my way around the buildings all over campus was much more of an overwhelming ordeal for me!

I couldn't find the buildings that several of my classes were in. Lots of times I had to just miss class because even the days I finally managed to find the class it was almost over. I didn't know what was worse, going in super late or just not going in at all. When I missed class I would just find my way to the library and read a chapter from that class's text book.

---

[28] Helen Keller US blind & deaf educator (1880-1968)

When I first walked in my massively large math classroom, I couldn't believe the size of the auditorium. There were about 400 students in the class. I had contact lenses so I could see well but still couldn't sit too far from the front of the room or I wouldn't be able to good enough to take notes off the gigantic chalk board. Of course I didn't want to get called on by the professor either but if I did I would always just say "I don't know" and he could find plenty of other students that would answer his questions. No one knew me and I didn't think the professor would ever know me either.

Those scholarships were used up fast. I was running out of the cash I saved up quickly so I started working at the cafeteria from 6 am until 9 am every morning. I knew that I wasn't there (living in that college town) to work but I liked having a job for several reasons. When I was at work in the cafeteria it took my mind off all my problems with school. So to say it another way, it took my mind off why I was there in first place. There was no question that I had to work to have money but I also loved the escape it gave me. I had a lot of fun working in that cafeteria kitchen and working with my boss who was the head chef. He had to train me on how to use the kitchen equipment and all the rules we had to follow when cooking and cleaning during our shift. My job was to make about 300 pancakes every morning. It took me a while to learn how to flip every single pancake on the huge grill before they all burned. My boss and I laughed a lot, I also liked the music he played on his little radio and he thought I was so funny.

My classes were so hard that I couldn't even understand enough to be able to take notes. I didn't expect myself to do well but I still kept trying like a silly fool. Also, I didn't understand enough about what the professor was saying to write down one sentence that hardly made any sense to me. I scribbled a bunch of three letter phrases in my notebook. When I got back to my dorm and looked over my notes it didn't say anything that I could study from so I was stuck with looking over the whole chapter and it was so boring that I would start to fall asleep after reading the second paragraph.

I wasn't interested in the information I was supposed to read. Besides, I never did homework growing up so it wasn't fun for me to force myself to sit down to the class assignments.

It wasn't too big of a surprise to see that I was failing my classes and college was too hard for me. But even still, when I finally accepted the fact that I wasn't going to pass my classes the first semester, I have to admit, I was excited about the fact that I could take the classes all over again in the Spring and have a head start on the other kids because it would be familiar to me.

> *It is hard to fail, but it is worse never to have tried to succeed.*
> *—Theodore Roosevelt*

The first semester went by really fast. As I said, the campus was huge. It was like a mini-city. Just about the time I knew my way all around campus, wouldn't you know the semester was totally over?

Second semester started and things didn't work out at all like I expected! For me it wasn't much different than taking the classes for the first time all over again.

I was definitely ashamed of my failure. However, I felt like regardless of how things turned out I experienced college life in a dorm and in a college town and did what I dreamed of doing. After that year I packed up and moved back home.

I went back to school, working during the day and going to school at night. I started going to the free tutor labs and they helped me understand the sections of the class lessons that I struggled with. Mostly I used the tutor labs for my math classes. By going straight to the tutor lab after class and practicing what I had just learned helped me a great deal and when I took the exams I was able to pass with good grades. I finally earned a Business Degree.

In 1994, Lindsey did a lot of research and found a way to send a letter to Dad. He finally responded and had his letter routed from Japan to

California to Texas. Dad and his wife had been living in Japan this whole time, we had heard from his relative that he had lots of new children with his wife but we weren't sure how many. We all read his letter, and it gave us chills. It was like reading something that came from a ghost. It was hard to believe that we actually received something from him. He was so protective about his privacy. We didn't even feel that his letter was really written from him and we did not feel good about it. We ended up not keeping in touch with him.

Dad's letter to Lindsey:

> Dear Lindsey,
>
> Thank you so much for the call that you placed to our family home in California in hopes of locating me and speaking with me personally. I appreciate very much the fact that you are trying to renew contact with me, and that means a lot to me. I've since received word of your call and am getting back to you here in a letter, which I've asked the family members there in Texas to personally deliver to you. You might think it's a bit odd that I wouldn't return your call with a call, being that telephone calls are quite easy and quick in this day and age, and can be placed from anywhere around the world, and that distance or time should not be a barrier. You may also wonder why it's taken so long to get a response from your father, and I hope, Honey, to be able to explain as best as I can in this letter to you, why you're hearing back from me now somewhat delayed and via a letter, for my initial response. I guess you can imagine, dear Lindsey, after not seeing you for fourteen years, you or the other children and your mother, that I'm a bit overwhelmed at this point, even as to what to say and certainly how to say it.
>
> (See appendices for the complete letter.)

Mom was working and raising the kids that were still living at home. Lindsey was living with her husband and started a family. I was out on my own.

My brothers and sisters all worked at some kind of job (boys would deliver newspaper and mow people's yard and girls would babysit and work somewhere after school), we all learned that if you work for something you get something that you would not have had otherwise. Also, we were learning that when faced with obstacles and disappointments we had to handle it with mind over matter and somehow push ourselves forward.

It is good to have goals and learn how to obtain them, some goals make up who we are and if we never obtain them we will always wish we did.

All of us were learning that our failures were part of the bigger picture of understanding where we came from, finding our place and setting goals for tomorrow.

The boys were all growing up. Andretti was still the leader except now he was protecting them whenever they got into trouble with other kids. Our brothers were all athletic and had friends but growing up as a kid is not easy, especially when you don't have a dad.

One day Andretti and Sebastian Jr. were walking to the corner store and ran into a "little" trouble on the way back. Just as they left the store and got on the sidewalk they heard somebody trying to get their attention. The voice was coming from behind the building, it sounded like a thuggish kind of voice;

"Say man, hey white boy hold up fool"

Andretti and Sebastian Jr. looked at each other and Andretti said keep walking. The voice turned into two voices and it was obviously getting closer. Then they noticed a couple scary thugs walking towards them in an aggressive way. My brothers immediately stopped and went *back to back*!

Sebastian Jr. said;

"Shit man there's at least 5!"

Andretti responded;

"Don't do anything, I got it"

In seconds my brothers were surrounded by 5 gangster type punks talking *smack* to them. Andretti immediately went ape wild, he started jumping up and down like a crazy man boxer. He was smiling and laughing at the gangster guys. He said;

"WHAT THE HELL, you WANNA mess with me?

Come on! I'll mess you up so bad, you pieces of shit!"

Then Andretti told Sebastian Jr.;

"Sebastian, GO get the boys! Grab Tony and Vitto, it's on baby! We're gonna kill these stupid ass losers!"

All the thugs were looking around at each other, they were in shock. Sebastian Jr. was shocked most of all! He looked at Andretti and said;

"WHAT!"

Andretti then started pushing Sebastian Jr. away saying;

"I said go get the boys!

We're gonna cremate them! They have no idea how freakin crazy we are!

Go, run, Go!"

Sebastian Jr. was scared but he was ready to fight. Andretti then threw down the things he was holding and violently ripped off his shirt. The thugs looked scared to death and started saying;

"Yo! Cool it Man!" "Hey, Look . . ."

Andretti got even louder and kept acting crazy. The thugs started backing up. Then Sebastian Jr. started running toward the direction of the way back home screaming;

"Hell Yeah! Let's mess these punks up,

I'm bringing the boys back right now so we can kill these shit head scum bags!"

Once Sebastian Jr. got as far as a block down the road he stopped and turned right back around. As he was walking he saw Andretti walking towards his direction with their things in his hands. Andretti was walking like nothing happened. He told Sebastian that he was mad at him for not leaving right away when he first told him to leave.

It is a good thing Andretti had heroic stories to go back and tell Mom, it probably helped out when he got into real trouble with her.

For a short while when Andretti was a teenager he started taking advantage of Mom and having his friends stay over for the night all the time. At night after Mom went to bed they would eat all the food in the refrigerator and mess up the living room. That wasn't the worst part. When Mom would get in her car in the morning and start the engine, it would be totally out of gas!

Mom felt safer with Andretti being home than at his friend's house so she decided to take a couple precautions with Andretti. Before she went to bed she chained the refrigerator door with a lock. She also opened the hood of the car and unplugged several wires so he couldn't start the car.

When there was bad news at home there always seemed to be some good news right around the corner. Our baby sisters, Madeline and Annabelle were growing up fast. We adored them; they were like two peas in a pod. Even though they were over three years apart they played together and were good friends growing up like Lindsey and I.

One year Madeline and Annabelle told Mom they wanted to be in the talent show dancing the Jitterbug. We all helped them move the furniture out of the way in the living room so they could practice. Mom, Emily and Stefano practiced with them for days and hours. Mom made them matching black and white petticoat polka dot dresses. We watch them practice a lot but once they learned the Jitterbug they put on a "formal" performance for us all. They were amazing and we had a lot of fun watching them. In the contest they danced to *Rock Around the Clock* by Bill Haley and the Comets and the Won!

**Madeline and Annabelle after winning the talent show dancing the
Jitterbug to *Rock Around the Clock* by Bill Haley and the Comets**

CHAPTER 14

Meeting Dad After a 17 Year Absence

1998 Dallas, Texas

We had last seen Dad in 1981. Emily had developed a drug problem, and it got worse over time. It got to the point where her drug problem was so bad we thought we were going to lose her. We tried everything we could to help, but her addiction was much more powerful than anything we could do or say. After exhausting all options, we were desperate and Lindsey reached out to Dad once again.

Lindsey had not tried to locate my Dad since the last time in 1994. She did research on the Internet and first got in touch with someone who knew him. She explained our situation with my sister, and this person got the message to Dad and he wrote Lindsey back. Lindsey immediately responded.

Lindsey's e-mail to Dad August 1998;

1998

Dear Dad:

Thank you for responding to my letter. Obviously I have
a great deal to share with you about the past 17 years
of our lives without you. However, as you can probably
understand I am fearful of how you might respond to

me. When you left to be with The Family, you left a black hole of emotional and traumatic trials for us to deal with. We are survivors of a bloody emotional war. And as much as I am dying to share my life with you, I am not interested in inviting a postwar looter into my heart only to leave me empty again. I would like for you to e-mail me a recent photo of yourself. I would like to know about your health. I would like for you to share with me some of the memories of our past life together. Can you tell me what our address was in Cuernavaca? What are the dates and birth of your children with my mother? As far as Emily is concerned, she has suffered more than any person I know. She has been doing horrible drugs, and I don't know exactly for how long. It is sickening to see her destroy her own life. She has a little boy. He is four and the most intelligent child on earth. At the moment, Emily is under Mom's care, and she is able to visit her boy. But I don't know how long this will last. This battle with Emily's drug addiction has exhausted and drained all of us to the point that we are almost ready to let go of her.

(See appendices for full letter.)

In August of 1998, Mom held a family meeting so we could talk about our feelings regarding Dad coming back to visit. We planned for each of us to talk about how we felt and we were going to decide as a family if we really wanted him to come back.

We needed to make sure we wanted to reopen that door. We video recorded the family meeting. Each one of us felt very differently about the whole idea. We were all different ages when we last saw Dad and had very different memories of our life with him. We all felt abandoned by him, and the fact that he was not "the one trying to find us" and be in our lives was reason enough for us not to want him back. AND, we found out he had eight new children with his second wife, and we felt like he didn't ever try to find us because he *had* replaced us. You can imagine how we all felt. We wished we didn't even know the truth, that way we could just go on like we had for 17 years thinking about him and believing that we would see him again one day.

Regardless, we had a family emergency with Emily and thought that maybe Dad's return could save her life, and were desperate for his help. We all agreed that we needed Dad's help, so in late August of 1998 Dad came to Dallas and met all of us for the first time in seventeen years.

Dad arrived from Japan at night. Mom and Lindsey picked him up from the airport and the rest of us were waiting at a Mexican restaurant. We chose Mexican because it represented the wonderful times we had in Mexico with him. Mom and Lindsey walked into the restaurant first and we were all looking around for him. We wondered if he still had hair on his head, we wondered if he was shorter, we wondered if he was fat or skinny, and if he still had his big smile.

Dad saw us and walked up to the table. I wish I had a picture of the looks on our faces.

Life stood completely still.

Our hearts completely sank—this was the moment we had been waiting for and thinking about for 17 years.

We always had a feeling like we would see him one day.

We went through the emotions of,

"Oh my God, it's Dad!"

We held our breath for a few seconds. Then we felt all the years pass by and it hit us like a ton of bricks. He looked totally different. We had expected to see the Dad we saw seventeen years ago. He was much older and had a humble, weak smile. He looked around at us, and I don't think he knew which one of my brothers was Stefano and which one was Sebastian Jr., but he recognized Andretti and Luigio. With a broken, quiet voice he said,

"Hi."

Then he looked around and with an even quieter voice, he slowly called out our names. He said,

"Hi . . . Sophia . . . ah . . .

Hi . . . Emily, umm . . .

Andretti,

Luigio,

Hi Sebastian,

Hello Stefano.

Some of us said hi back and some of us did not say a word.

Stefano was only a toddler when Dad left, and Sebastian Jr. was also young, but we always talked about Dad.

I can't speak for how they felt. But I believe when they saw Dad, they didn't remember him.

They were very polite and proud and shook Dad's hand—Sebastian Jr. first, then Stefano.

They did not have all the good *and* bad memories of him that we did. In a way, they were robbed of that. The older children experienced a different kind of emotional sadness than the younger children.

Immediately we all had bloodshot eyes.

We were emotionally drained and tears came running down our faces. We felt distant from him, and seeing him was overwhelmingly surreal.

Dad's visit was a little over a week. It was enough time to give everyone a chance to see him and not too much time for us to be anxious for him to fly back to Japan. We all needed to unravel our emotions, have our space and digest the fact that we had just seen him after all these years of absence in our life.

He traveled back to Japan where he and his new family of nine children were living with the COG cult. There were a few e-mails that went back and forth after his return to Japan. First with Lindsey, then with Mom, and ultimately he wrote one e-mail on October 2, 1998.

His e-mail said:

> Dear Lindsey, Sophia, Emily, Andretti, Luigio,
> Sebastian, Stefano,

> I love you all so very much and cannot express what
> a wonderful answer to prayer it has been for me to
> now be able to love you again, and be in very close
> communications with you all. We are only beginning
> to meld together in heart, mind, and soul, and I believe
> that the future for us (though a big mysterious at
> present) will be a happy and exciting one! Thank you for
> taking me into your arms again! Did I tell you enough,
> in all our beautiful times of heart-sharing together, how
> very much I love and need each one of you? As I sit
> here now in my little office before beginning my day,
> the memory of you all and the two brief weeks we've
> just spent together seems like a dream. Though very
> tangible, the effect that your loving touch has had on
> my life is still almost too good to be true! Thank you for
> being all that you are to me, your grateful father!

> (See appendices for full letter.)

**Family meeting Dad in a Mexican restaurant in Texas
after his arrival from Japan**

CHAPTER 15

"Don't wait for the opportunities in life. Create them!"

(Flash Forward to Present Day)

My Family . . . . The way we are . . .

Is it because;

> *We burned up the record player with "I Will Survive" by Gloria Gaynor?*
>
> *We earned our stripes from our overly optimistic drill sergeant mom?*
>
> *We had too many Soul Train simulations at home in the 1980s?*
>
> *We were always chasing after something growing up?*
>
> *We learned how to "fight for yourself"?*
>
> *We learned what it's like to take a chance at your dream even if you think you might fail?*

We know what it's like to fail, but then succeed?

We were all bit by a snake or a Jitterbug?

We ate too many crawfish or chicharrones?

We grew up surrounded with vibrant, feisty and shy personalities?

We learned growing up that a parent should teach their children to be considerate and caring of others?

Our dad Sebastian, his wife, and their nine children have moved back to United States and are all very close. Dad and his wife admit the toxic aftermath the COG had on everyone's life. They renounced their faith and belief in the COG cult, and now Dad is picking up the pieces.

Our mom Elizabeth dedicates her life to supporting her children and spending quality time alone with her thirteen grandchildren. She has written several children's storybooks, and her grandchildren love to hear her read them. She hopes to get them published soon. She always makes time to get together with her children, just like she has always done. She travels to California to visit Andretti, Sebastian Jr., and Annabelle. She travels to Colorado to visit Madeline. Luigio lives mostly in Central America, but stays at Mom's house when he comes back to paint murals. Fortunately Lindsey, Emily, Stefano, and I live in the same town and can get together often.

Mom has a successful interior design business and continues to receive word-of-mouth referrals for her creative, one-of-a-kind work. She works very hard at her business. Luigio is one of the artists that she hires to complete mural paintings. Mom's clients love her work and comment that they have never seen personalized work quite like hers. She has many regrets for the life we once lived and what she says are the horrible choices she made. But we don't see it that way. She remains a wonderful parent, and we respect her for who she is. Mom refers to the old sayings, "When God gives us lemons, we make lemonade" and "Look on the bright side of life, our cup is always at least half full if not overflowing." Our family gets together often. Mom always cooks several huge dinners for us all at her home, Christmas dinner is one of her most special dinners. We have lots of fun getting together during the holidays.

Poem written by Stefano for Mom,
THE RADDEST MOM
Sometimes I think your brain is made of gummies
But then I realize you had to fill 9 tummies
When times were hard, you were even harder
Doing anything necessary, slave, hustle and barter
Your family driven goal have raised the bar
For caring Mothers all over, near and far
The sacrifices you've made haven't gone unseen
Your friends and your family know what I mean
Because of you we can now blossom and grow
The future is bright and we're ready to go
Things can only get better we've learned from your ways
When you put in your all you get out of the maze
I'll end this poem with a promising look ahead
Thanks to my Mother it's onward we will tread.

Lindsey Star was so involved with her first two boys throughout their whole lives and embraced life to the fullest. She wrote many beautiful songs about her family and our family. She sang at my wedding and I was so proud to have her as my matron of honor. Lindsey also sang at several of our families' weddings as well as various charity functions over the past fifteen years. She has done every art project that one can think of, such as sewing, cooking, and sculpture. She has a wonderful husband named John and they have been together for over twenty years. Lindsey dedicated herself full-time to being a wife and mother. Shortly thereafter, she founded her industrial equipment Company.

Emily Knight now lives with Mom and still gets up early every morning to make her coffee. She has followed Mom in her desire and love for fashion and she is very talented with an eye for stylish clothing and interior decor. Emily is a caring and gentle person with a beautiful smile and a special cute laugh. She helps mom with her interior design projects. Emily also likes to spend time with my family and when she is with us it is such a treat. She helps me cook and do special fun things with the kids. I love having her visit us!

Her favorite thing to do in the world is hanging out with her son, Andy. He is handsome and has a most beautiful polite and considerate personality. He is currently an honor roll student in high school and making his plans for college.

Andretti (my 5 year old birthday gift) has traveled all over and his passion drove him to pursue different careers. He settled down with a beautiful wife. He is a writer at heart and has written about his experiences and our life growing up. He recently wrote a story about Mom. He and his wife settled down in a home that allows them to enjoy the things in life they love to do, like cooking, walking on the beach, and developing their career as artists. He's always taking up new sports and now he spends at least ten hours a week surfing. He said it is the most fun he's ever had and promised to make me a video of him riding a wave. I look forward to talking to him over the phone, we can talk for hours.

Luigio has been focused on his self-taught artistic abilities. He can play almost any musical instrument he touches. His guitar music is the most beautiful music I have ever heard someone play live, but he has never pursued it as a career. We love the way he plays Andres Segovia's music and Spanish guitar. I love his murals and hope one day he will give me a good deal and create a beautiful mural in our home. When he is not working, he travels the world. He stays in foreign countries for several months out of the year. The last few years he's made a home for himself in Central America where he studies art and has his own art gallery. When he travels back home, he is always wearing brightly colored clothes, and he has a beard and long hair. He loves to run a minimum of 4 miles a day. When his body is achy he walks 6 miles. He has a particular pallet for "all natural" foods. It doesn't bother him to grocery shop for hours to find the special natural ingredients he needs then spend another two hours preparing his meals.

He can be a little quiet and seem shy, but when he strikes up a conversation with you, he gives you an intelligent perspective on things that you would have never thought of. He still has his angelic smile. When he was a teenager he started to do creative artwork at school and he played the guitar; he was our only brother to take an interest in the guitar as a teenager. Luigio would kid around with us just before he started to play, but we couldn't wait for him to strike his fingers and play his chords because his music sounded so pleasant.

Sebastian Jr. has had a career in the retail business for over fifteen years. He currently manages a computer retail store in California. He has the most delightful personality, always dresses fashionably and loves to interact with everyone he meets. And by the way, he is very handsome, like my other three brothers. No one is a stranger to him, and everyone seems to like him or love him. When we all get together, he has the most hilarious stories to tell us about customers in his stores. He tells stories with such animated expressions that he has us falling down to the ground laughing.

For example, one morning he went to his store to open for the day. He opened the front door and noticed an envelope on the floor that had been slipped through the front door by a customer overnight. He picked it up and it had a postage stamp on it and had "Manager" written in fancy cursive on the front of the envelope—nothing else. He opened the letter and immediately saw it was addressed;

To: "Your Falt."

It did not say "Dear Sir" or "To Whom it May Concern," oh, and *fault* was misspelled. With Sebastian Jr.'s first natural reaction he instantly cracked up laughing. He told us that he continued to read the letter and it said;

"I dont get *celiar* in my house I worked for the fire department for 25 years, and I pay good money for my *celiar*, you're *falt*!"

Sebastian Jr. told us he got a good laugh out of it and that was how he started his morning that day. That's the way Sebastian is, he has a great sense of humor so when he has to deal with very difficult customers, on the surface he handles it professionally but on a personal level he is entertained by some of the crazy things people say and do and he finds the daily challenges it all brings is fascinating. His customers also really like him, his genuine friendly smile and personality wins them over. He has so many stories like this and it makes the family visits so much fun. During our family gatherings his stories also set the mood for the rest of us sharing our funny stories and experiences. When we get together it makes "today" feel just like old times!

Sebastian Jr. has a passion for all sorts of sports, especially basketball. He plays basketball as often as he can and over the years has made so many friends playing and tells the funniest *basketball stories*. But also he has had so many injuries like breaking his nose, hurting his ankles and knees but he has always recovered and still loves to play.

Since Andretti and Sebastian Jr. live close to each other, they get together all the time to surf. They say it is beautiful in California, and they're outside all the time. They surf, play basketball, and have cookouts. He has recently taken up art as well, and has created some amazing paintings.

Stefano joined a martial arts school when he was twelve years old. To this day, he still practices martial arts and has become a master and teacher. We enjoyed watching his competitions over the years and to watch his dedication and discipline with his martial arts. Stefano earned a business degree, and while in college he received special recognition for an entrepreneur business program.

He has a beautiful wife who helps him with the family business and three adorable children. His first daughter was born just seven weeks before my daughter. They are two peas in a pod when they are together. Stefano joined Lindsey's industrial equipment business as her partner.

Madeline has two beautiful boys, three step-daughters and a great husband. She manages a turbine machinery service business in Colorado. Her life is full of passion, laughter, optimism, and love for her family. She moved from Texas to pursue her career, did some theater work as a part-time actress, and studied martial arts with her two sons. She worked very hard as a single mom before she met the man of her dreams. Madeline enrolled in college and is studying to be a psychologist. Her husband, Michael, has his own business. They are very busy co-parenting their 5 children and managing their careers. Colorado is a beautiful place to live, they always make time to do things like cycle, ski and go on hiking trails.

Annabelle, after taking four years of ROTC in high school, served in the U.S. Air Force for four years in Germany as a radiology technician, and helped to provide medical assistance to our wounded soldiers. Even though she is the youngest of nine children and we spoiled her rotten, she has never asked for anything and has always been independent. She has a beautiful two-year-old daughter and is an excellent mother. She is pursuing a degree and career as a court reporter in California in order to provide a better life and future for daughter. She loves her family and comes to visit us all in Texas as often as she can; she also goes to visit Madeline in Colorado.

Ever since we met our cousin Lynn when we first returned to the U.S. (when I was eleven), she's been part of our lives. She has a wonderful husband named Joseph. They always come to our family weddings, birthdays, and holiday parties. They don't have any children, but they love spending the weekends with us and spending time with our two children.

As for me, at thirty-six, I decided that a family was just not in the cards for me. Shortly after that I received an unexpected blessing and became a wife and mother. I was fortunate enough to have our wonderful Uncle Bob give me away at my wedding. My wedding was like a fairy tale wedding. It really wasn't our intention for it to be so perfect, it just was! Mom was by my side, she made me a beautiful wedding dress just like the traditional wedding styles I always loved as a young girl. Lindsey was my matron of honor; my sisters and my cousin Lynn were my bridesmaids. Our beloved Uncle Bob passed away a couple of years ago, but his twin sister Martha is living a fulfilling life with her husband and their children and grandchildren.

I am blessed with a wonderful husband, Jeff. We were friends for a couple years and after several failed attempts to set him up with my single girlfriends, we surprised each other and came up with the idea to go on a date. We have been together ever since. He is an excellent daddy and is relentlessly patient with me. In a loving way, he laughs at my mistakes and shortcomings. He is an only child but adores large families. We grew up so differently and yet we agree on most of the things that are the common problems for couples. We're fortunate that our children have caring and available grandparents who come over often (thank God; I *really* have great in-laws).

The best part about him is that he is grounded, consistent, and confident. His character is honorable, and he is always courteous and kind to everyone. After almost a decade working in public accounting, I was ready for an industry change. I went to work for a large oil and gas company, and I am now in my eleventh year with the company. Our children are our biggest blessing. I was thirty-six when I was pregnant with my first child (William) and had a great, healthy pregnancy.

Two years after my son was born, Lindsey's boys were seventeen and eighteen, and she became pregnant with twin boys. Right after that, I became pregnant with our sweetheart daughter (Lori). During the entire pregnancy with my daughter, I rode my bike after work. I would put my son in the baby seat attached to my bike, and we would get some exercise. I had a wonderful pregnancy my daughter, just like I had with my son.

I struggle like everyone else to balance having a family and full-time career. I have visions of being in my crowded childhood home hearing, "Mom, Mom, hey Mom, Look, watch this, Mom." I miss my awesome brothers and sisters and all the fun we used to have growing up. When I hear my two babies say, "Mom, Mom" and look down and see their beautiful sweet faces light up with their inquisitive eyes, my heart melts. Children say the cutest things. The other day my six-year-old son said, "Mom, can we get a television in my room? The reason why is so that when I'm grounded to my room, I'll have something to do." I thought that was so funny! I guess he doesn't realize that he's not supposed to be entertained when he's grounded.

Last summer when my daughter was three, her Nana (my mother-in-law married to my father-in-law) was acting like she was about to step into her bathing suit, and said "Lori, can I wear your bathing suit"? My daughter said, "No Nana you can't. You're too big, but that's okay because you can wear it when you get small like me," and she had a precious look on her face. She didn't want to disappoint her Nana! I feel so lucky to have my own family.

No doubt I struggle with keeping focus and balance in life. The biggest challenge is using good judgment, especially when both my career, that I've built for over 20 years and truly enjoy, and family require my focus and attention. I'm so lucky to have an adorable 4 year old daughter, 6 year old amazing son and husband that are perfect for me.

One thing is for sure, our fellowship together continues to enrich our lives!

We continue to inspire each other and cherish the times we manage to get together. Each of us don't think of ourselves as having great accomplishments, but when we talk to each other over the phone or visit in person, we find ourselves surprised at how proud we are of what we have accomplished in our lives.

APPENDICES

(Poems, songs and letters)

Poems Lindsey wrote:

1988 (Lindsey's Poem)

Dear Dad,
It's been a long time I hardly know how to begin.
You're on my mind day and night.
In my haunting dreams,
I endlessly ponder what is right. What is right?
I don't know. Why did you have to go?
The day you left me, I was just a kid, doubting your flee,
was it something I did?
I see you each night in a vision when I fall asleep,
I run to you with open arms but aborted love awakes me,
and I weep in my dreams.
I pour out my heart to you in desperation,
but when I wake I am left empty:
no answers only dissolution.
Hopelessly I dream,
still I cannot change this plot,
endlessly I search to find the love that is not.
You are gone now, and I don't doubt that anymore,
but that doesn't change the fact that my heart has stayed sore.
It's too bad you didn't get to see me grow up.
I'm a married woman now,
and expecting my first pup.
I hear that Japan is where you abide,
but even halfway around the world,
your conscience cannot hide.
I know you're thinking,

175

"Your mind is like mine."
So, get out your pen and write me a line.

1988 (Lindsey's Poem)
*"**We** have been below poverty,*
but we have always been fed.
We have been without a home,
but we always had a bed.
One person was there to wipe away the tears.
She loved us and helped us get over our fears.
She held up the fort and pulled us all through.
Mom did the job you were supposed to do.
One person was always there,
but it was never you."

1994 (Lindsey's Poem)
*"**Where** is my Daddy?"*
She would often hear,
from wondering little faces standing so near.
I don't really know,
and I can't explain but he's gone away and life is full of change.
But will he be back?
I thought that he cared.
Please tell me Mommy,
now I'm getting scared.
Maybe it's my fault,
I did something wrong.
Well, I'm sorry but he is still gone.
No Daddy to love us,
tickle and chase us,
our daddy has left us and tried to erase us.

Poem written by Stefano;

Poem written by Stefano (Present Day),

THE RADDEST MOM

Sometimes I think your brain is made of gummies
But then I realize you had to fill 9 tummies

When times were hard, you were even harder
Doing anything necessary, slave, hustle and barter

Your family driven goal have raised the bar
For caring Mothers all over, near and far

The sacrifices you've made haven't gone unseen
Your friends and your family know what I mean

Because of you we can now blossom and grow
The future is bright and we're ready to go

Things can only get better we've learned from your ways
When you put in your all you get out of the maze

I'll end this poem with a promising look ahead
Thanks to my Mother it's onward we will tread.

Songs written by Lindsey Star (1984-2003)

Perfect Love By Lindsey Star—
2001 (Sophia's favorite song)

How can I thank you, for your love
How can I praise you, for your faithfulness
In you I have peace, through you I am free
and you fill me from the fountain of your perfect love
And you give me a reason to rise above
And in your spirit I am renewed
And in your divine presence
I am complete . . . completely yours
How can I serve you, show me your way
I want to be sensitive to your desires, I am yours
In you I have peace,
through you I am free
And you give me a reason to rise above
And in your spirit I am renewed
And in your divine presence
I am complete . . . completely yours

A Real Woman By Lindsey Star
(written about Elizabeth-1984)

Have you ever know a real woman? Heart of rubies, soul of passion . . .
Let me tell you about this woman I love
She is a woman of many qualities,
She's a woman who's never hard to please
Her life is worth, it's worth more than gold,
Stories of here have many times been told
She has carried 9 children next to her heart,
That she'll love forever and they'll never part
She has planned and provided and made them a life
She's fought and struggled and taught them how to survive
She's a mother and a father and a teacher in one
When things got down, she said look toward the sun
And we did . . .
And we lived

Unbroken by Lindsey Star (2003)

Human flesh and spirit, woven to become,
filled with life and purpose, for the journey yet to come
Human intuition, leads our hearts to form dreams,
of what we can imagine, our life supposed to be.
But the future is undetermined, and what's made perfect is fragile still
And there's no understanding when the dreams we've imagined are
broken . . .
When what we've known is no longer whole or real, but broken
and we are left with pieces, and a world of empty spaces
Still this life continues to unfold, it's simple beauty before our eyes,
but we filter it through the pieces of stained glass within our minds
But enchanted are the possibilities, of human spirit, woven to become
a continuous renewing of life that remains Unbroken . . .
When what we've known survives to live again,
Unbroken . . .
and we are left with pieces of a lifetime, to begin again

Dear Dad By Lindsey Star (1995)

This is to your dear dad, it's been a long time, I hardly know . . .
how to begin . . . you on my mind, day and night
In my haunting dreams, endlessly ponder what is right . . .
What is right?
I don't know, why did you have to go and leave your family
and I was just a kid, doubting your flee . . . Was it something I did?
I see you each night in a vision when I fall asleep,
I run to you with open arms, but aborted love awakes me and I weep
Why did you have to go? I am full of emotions, that I cannot explain,
my heart and my soul have nothing to gain
Stefano's a big boy now
Sebastian Jr.'s a man and he looks just like you
Luigio is an artist who think's life is too complex
and Andretti's going to be the next James Dean
Emily's on her own, trying to make it in this world
Sophia's going to earn a business degree
And I'm a mother now, with 2 precious little boys,
And I never gave up hoping that one day we might share the joy.
This is to you dear dad, it's been such a long long time,
I hardly know . . .
You on my mind, day and night, and I in my haunting dreams,
endlessly ponder what is right. Oh what is right . . . Dad?
What is right dad?
What is right dad?
What is right dad?
What is right dad?

Overcome By Lindsey Star (1998)

A girl became a woman before she knew she was her own
Told she should be rescued, from the fate of being alone
And she gave him 7 children and he gave her the living room floor
As he sang and preached the bible, he banged the girl next door
And she said, who will be my lover
And who will feed my lambs
Will I die here in this modern hell
Will I see the promised land
Will God send me a savior,
Will he send his only son?
If this is the life I was born to live,
Then I must overcome
The many thirsty years she lived led her to understand
That if she was ever to find love, it would not be in a man
And when she reached the age of wisdom, her life became her own
She found the key to unlock her spirit and the freedom to be alone
And she said, I will be my lover
and I will feed my lambs
I will live here in the life I choose
and I will see the promised land
I am free from the lies and darkness
and my world has just begun
This is the life I was born to live,
and I have overcome

Always Strong for Me
(written for her husband John-2003)
By Lindsey Star

Do you know, how much, you mean to me?
And do I tell you how much I really care?
You're always there, always care, always strong for me!
And through the years, I've come to know one thing . . .
That I am so in love with you, and you mean the world to me
Your strong arms offer me a place to rest my heart
Do you know I can feel the warmth, inside you
and when I look into your eyes, I see the love your feel for me
And I am so in love with you, and you mean the world to me
Your strong arms offer me a place to rest my heart . . .
My Love

So Close By Lindsey Star (1984)

A confused feeling is the worse that you can have
Lost in insecurity, not sure for what to grab
The loving warm closeness and sincerity of a friend
Can bring out your emotions and bring these feelings to and end
And you and I can be so close
We share our dreams and share our fears
And if a heart is hurt or broke
Together we can mend the tears
As friends, we can grow closer and our love with therefore grow strong
And we are free to confide and trust for these friends,
can never go wrong
And there may be obstacles that lie in the road,
but none too tough to defeat
And we will continue to bloom like a rose, and our essence,
increasingly sweet . . .
And you and I can be so close, we share our dreams and share our fears,
And if a heart is hurt or broke, together we can mend the tears . . .

1994 Letter from Sebastian (Dad) to Lindsey:

Dear Lindsey,

Thank you so much for the call that you placed to our family home in California in hopes of locating me and speaking with me personally. I appreciate very much the fact that you are trying to renew contact with me, and that means a lot to me. I've since received word of your call and am getting back to you here in a letter, which I've asked the family members there in Texas to personally deliver to you. You might think it's a bit odd that I wouldn't return your call with a call, being that telephone calls are quite easy and quick in this day and age, and can be placed from anywhere around the world, and that distance or time should not be a barrier. You may also wonder why it's taken so long to get a response from your father, and I hope, Honey, to be able to explain as best as I can in this letter to you, why you're hearing back from me now somewhat delayed and via a letter, for my initial response.

I guess you can imagine, dear Lindsey, after not seeing you for fourteen years, you or the other children and your mother, that I'm a bit overwhelmed at this point, even as to what to say and certainly how to say it. Since hearing about your call, I've been thinking and praying about just how to get back to you and what to say to you—how to express by any means the things that I feel and the things that I would want to communicate to you. As much as I would hope that renewing our contact together would be beautiful and positive, I'm certain that there must be a lot of unanswered questions, and a lot of feelings on your part, and on the part of all of my children and even your mother, that need to get out in the open and be expressed and shared, and, in most cases, I would imagine, reconciled. At this point, Honey, I don't really know so much about what you do feel and how you feel about your father, and the fact that we have not been together all of these years.

All I have to go on is a letter that you wrote me about seven years ago, which I must admit, was quite disturbing and I was hurt to see that you were hurt and had so many bad feelings, many of which I can understand were a natural way to react to your mother and my divorce and separation, and my leaving to go on with the family in full-time service to the Lord.

Being that you were a young teenager then, fourteen, I'm sure you must have had a lot of questions that needed to be answered. It was a difficult time for all of us, your mother included, and I admire how she's continued to care for you and be there for you all this time, even in the wake of the emotional disturbances that I'm sure must have resulted from all the changes that took place after I left and since that time. I want you to know, Lindsey, that a day has not gone by that I haven't thought of you and committed your care, your safety, and your health to the Lord for his help and protection. This may be of little comfort to you at this point. I don't know, but I would like to hear from you, just what your feelings are, and as much about you and what has happened in your life as you would like to tell me. I was around your age now at the time I left, about twenty-eight, so maybe in a way the difficulty or the struggle of having to handle the decisions that your mother and I had to handle at that time might be more relatable to you now, as I'm sure you've gone through many things in your own life. Anyway, I don't hope to clear all of that up in one letter, but I do want to let you know that I love you dearly, and I've always loved you. It has also been very difficult for me not being able to be in contact through the years, because of the circumstances that have led to many hard feelings on the part of your mother. Certainly I had a lot to do with that, being quite young, unwise, and inexperienced.

186

I know that I did not react well at the time or even in the years that followed, to being faced with divorce and the events that developed afterward. I'm sure that because of this, you suffered unnecessary hardship. I would very much like to hear from you, Lindsey, in more detail as to what you're doing and all about your life, your feelings, and anything that you'd like to write about after reading these different things from me, and anything you'd want to comment on. It would really help me to see more from your viewpoint, your feelings. I would appreciate that, and I promise to get back to you, too.

Lindsey, I'm going to ask, if you don't mind, that for now you would send me a letter via the family members there in Texas, as I am traveling now and do so quite regularly. This way, I'm sure that the letter will get to me safely and quickly. Of course, Lindsey, it would be thrilling for me to receive photos of you and your dear husband, along with your beautiful little boys. I would also love to hear from Sophia & Emily, Andretti, Luigio, Sebastian Jr. & Stefano, if they would want to write me. I wonder if you could just let them know that I'm not them directly because I don't know if they want to have contact with me. But if they want to, I would be very happy to hear from them, & Ill also answer them back. I don't know how your mother would feel about being in contact, or if she would even want to write a little something, but I would very much appreciate hearing from her as well, if she would like to communicate, I'll be looking forward to hearing from you!

Much Love,

Your Dad

Lindsey's email to Dad August 1998

Dear Dad:

Thank you for responding to my letter. Obviously I have a great deal to share with you about the past 17 years of our lives without you. However, as you can probably understand I am fearful of how you might respond to me. When you left to be with The Family, you left a black hole of emotional and traumatic trials for us to deal with. We are survivors of a bloody emotional war. And as much as I am dying to share my life with you, I am not interested in inviting a postwar looter into my heart only to leave me empty again. I would like for you to e-mail me a recent photo of yourself. I would like to know about your health. I would like for you to share with me some of the memories of our past life together. Can you tell me what our address was in Cuernavaca? What are the dates and birth of your children with my mother? As far as Emily is concerned, she has suffered more than any person I know. She has been doing horrible drugs, and I don't know exactly for how long. It is sickening to see her destroy her own life. She has a little boy. He is four and the most intelligent child on earth. At the moment, Emily is under Mom's care, and she is able to visit her boy. But I don't know how long this will last. This battle with Emily's drug addiction has exhausted and drained all of us to the point that we are almost ready to let go of her.

Mother suggested that I try to get a hold of you. I searched the Net, but to no avail. Two days after my failed attempts to locate a family address, I was stopped at a light and a young lady offered me a pamphlet. I accepted and gave a donation. I immediately called the 1-800 number on the back and gave my story. We are all uncertain that we have made the right choice to contact you. Our mother has fought tooth and nail to keep us all together, alive, and well so far.

She deserves a reward that has not yet been invented for the most courageous, determined single parent on the face of the planet. And out of respect for her and all she has contributed to our lives, I want to make damn sure that you are for real. I want to know that you will follow through with what you say you are going to do. I want to know that you really do care. I want you to prove it, and not just by praying for us from Japan. We all pray plenty for ourselves—how else could we have made it this far? I will look forward to your response on the issues of concern that I stated above.

Sincerely,

Your first child, Lindsey Star

Letter from Sebastian to us seven kids (1998):

Dear Lindsey, Sophia, Emily, Andretti,

Luigio, Sebastian, Stefano,

I love you all so very much and cannot express what a wonderful answer to prayer it has been for me to now be able to love you again, and be in very close communications with you all. We are only beginning to meld together in heart, mind, and soul, and I believe that the future for us (though a big mysterious at present) will be a happy and exciting one! Thank you for taking me into your arms again! Did I tell you enough, in all our beautiful times of heart-sharing together, how very much I love and need each one of you? As I sit here now in my little office before beginning my day, the memory of you all and the two brief weeks we've just spent together seems like a dream. Though very tangible, the effect that your loving touch has had on my life is still almost too good to be true! Thank you for being all that you are to me, your grateful father!

Well, as I mentioned to you before, I have now gotten set up with my own e-mail address and outside phone line from my little office. Since we are a big operation, I have not, up until now, been hands-on involved in the actual sending and receiving of e-mail or the many other phone communications that are received here on a daily basis. The Lord has been very good to me over the years and provided a secretary to help with such important, though time-consuming, daily duties here. However, at this auspicious juncture in my life, I'm determined to have a personal "hot line" with you, my family, so that our interaction during these formative days of our new life together is as seamless as possible, God willing! So all that to say, I'm now online, folks! Please feel free to drop me a note as you would like, and I will do my best to get back to you as soon as possible, okay? I love you!

Just to help you further understand how things work on this end—if you send me an e-mail, by 3:00 p.m. your time, I should be able to pick it up when I begin my morning quiet work (at 9:00 a.m. my time). If I receive your notes at this time, I can probably send you a reply right away, or soon after I read it. If your mail to me comes later in the day, I may not be able to get to it until the following day, as my work schedule is fairly full from 11:00 a.m. until 10:00 p.m. with meetings and counseling! Of course, any "Urgent" notes from you I can read and try to answer right away. Anyway, I hope that all of this helps you understand and feel closer to me during this next little while that we are separated by "time and tide." Please do try to keep in touch if you can! Looking forward to hearing from you!

Love Dad"